This is a sports book. It's a se. In fact, it's a book about life.

Division I men's college basketball referee Rick Hartzell shares life lessons from the court in *Whistle in a Haystack: A Farmboy's View on Life's Lessons, Leadership and College Basketball*. The journey he describes and the stories he tells cover more than basketball—they bring the reader a sense of what it's like to be in the game and all the things to ponder after the games are over.

From the intense play of top athletes to banter from well-known coaches like Bobby Knight, Mike Krzyzewski, Dean Smith, Roy Williams, and Bill Self, Hartzell brings you an inside view of a unique slice of life, one experienced by only a select few top officials in the U.S.

While running the hardwood from North Carolina to Iowa and California, Hartzell picked up lessons that every reader will find useful in his or her daily life, from how to deal with not getting the biggest assignment to knowing when and how to move on after a mistake.

This book is *must reading* for business leaders, and offers any reader powerful lessons from Hartzell's numerous on- and off-court experiences. Whether you are looking for a mentor or wish to become one, Hartzell has tips to help you along. If you want to build a stronger corporate team or just improve the camaraderie with your colleagues, Hartzell's insights will strengthen your ability to do so. If you want to be the best person/leader/dad you can be, the insights here give you new ideas to consider.

Hartzell partnered on the book with Dave Simon, an 18-year basketball officiating veteran who has written for *Referee Magazine* for over 25 years. With a foreword from the great Duke and Olympic coach Mike Krzyzewski, *Whistle in a Haystack* is a fun, interesting and easy read that gives tips to help you address personal or business obstacles in a format designed to share the learning experience long after you've put the book down.

Whistle in a Haystack

An Iowa Farmboy's View on Life's Lessons, Leadership, and College Basketball

Whistle in a Haystack

An Iowa Farmboy's View
on Life's Lessons, Leadership,
and College Basketball

Rick Hartzell
with Dave Simon

Library of Congress Control Number: 2015918199

FRONT AND BACK COVER PHOTO CREDIT
Christine Shea Robbins
Photography by Christine
319-352-0001

DEDICATION

I have always looked forward to writing this dedication for a book I hoped to write. I proudly dedicate this book to my mom and dad (Bob and Neva), who raised me and my sister, Jody, the right way by teaching us the value of hard work. We were poor but we didn't know it. We lived in an atmosphere of love and support. We were raised in a small farm house on 240 acres of mediocre Iowa farm land where you made your living by working hard. My parents never missed a game or a school event that I can remember. They loved each other and they loved me and my sister. They never fought. They loved. They encouraged me. They always had my back. After my dad died, my mom — the greatest mom of all time — let me go away to do what I needed and wanted to do. Not once did she say anything about me living in Iowa City, Chicago, Baltimore or Lewisburg. When I finally came back to Iowa to live, we lost mom. I loved them both, and thank them both, from the bottom of my heart. And, I miss them both, every single day.

I also want to dedicate this book to my sister, Jody. No one has ever had a better sister. She is loving, kind and just tough enough. She speaks her mind to me and tells me how it is. But, she loves and supports me in just the right way. I would give anything to be the person she is. Thank you, sis. You are the best. Jody's husband Steve is one of the most unselfish people — he would do anything for anyone. But, most important to me, he is my sister's best friend and soul mate — the coolest thing ever. They have raised Jess and Jay, two great young men. Way to go!

This book would not have been possible without my wife, Jill. She helped me start anew, a part of the process that ultimately led to getting this book written. I want to thank her for adding to my life and for helping me recognize that there are amazing second chapters to be written.

And, to my first wife, Kathy, I would like to thank you for the support you have given Nate and Amanda, our beautiful kids that we had together, and to me. I would not be on the path I am now without you.

And, I dedicate this book to my four kids Nate, Amanda, Jackson and Jace. You have been the light of my life; you have been my reason for living. I would do anything for any of you. We have come through some of life's trials and tribulations together and have come out the other side okay. We have so much love between us and a special bond. I'm an extremely lucky man to have four diverse kids, all of whom are unique and special in their own way. I wrote this book at least partially for all of you, to leave a legacy that you could read someday and so you would know that your dad loves you and cherishes you and is so proud of each of you. I hope we have a few more decades together. But when it ends and I am here no longer, please know that of all the things I was fortunate enough to do in my life, of all the places I went and the things I saw and experienced, **<u>nothing in the world is more important to me, nor has had more of a positive and life-changing impact on me than the four of you.</u>**

You are my pride and joy, my inspiration, my reason for living. I love all of you with all my heart. You inspire me every day to do the best I can. You give me a reason to go on and work hard and try to do better each day, even when life gets hard. And, in the end, all I want is for you to be proud of your dad. Because he is so enormously proud of each of you. And, I want each of you to carry on this Hartzell name, in the very best and most positive way that you can, when I am gone. You each have a unique story to tell; Nate, getting you out of where you were born is the most special thing I have ever done, and because of that you have had a chance to make a great life, which you have done; Amanda, they said we could not have a baby and here you came. What a blessing. You are so tough and so resilient and so talented; how many thousands of jump shots did we shoot together? Jackson, my dear Jackson. Who would have thought that you would ever come along? I was skeptical, I was too old to be a dad again. You have been the most special and inspiring young man to me. We have spent more days and hours together than any dad and son ever and I would not trade that for anything; and Jace, you came along at just the right time, you are beautiful and it is my job to stay healthy and strong to help raise you into a special young man.

Jackson, my 9-year-old son, has been so important to me over the past few years for so many reasons. We are great friends. I am his coach and his friend and he is mine. He has lifted me up when I was down. He tells me he loves me every single day. And he respects me and knows that dads have to be tough sometimes. I have had more time to give to him, given the stage of my life that I am in now. You are a talented boy and I will do all I can to help you develop that talent as a student, a person and perhaps, as an athlete.

One night I was on the road refereeing and I called Jackson after the game. He said to me, "Dad I love you all the way up to the moon and sky and milky way and sun and 'gravitytation' and as big as the world and as big as your heart and bigger than anything." Enough said. I feel the same way, pal. That is a lot of love. 6 4 9 18 23. ■

Rick Hartzell
November 2015

TABLE OF CONTENTS

Foreword from Mike Krzyzewski

At Duke University, we work hard to develop leadership qualities in our student-athletes. Over the years, I've been fortunate to coach and help many players in the men's basketball program refine their skills and help them learn how to assist the next generation to better understand and lead them in the world in which we live.

"Leadership" is a word that also defines Rick Hartzell. Leadership doesn't come easy, and it's not inherent. Rick has worked hard at his basketball officiating over the past 35 years to reach a level of sustained excellence. That's evident in the number of high level Men's Division I NCAA basketball and NCAA tournament games he's worked, the relationships he's built with his fellow officials, supervisors and administrators, and the respect he has from coaches.

Whistle in a Haystack is Rick's leadership message, but much, much more. This book is about character, teamwork, personal growth and, indeed, life in general. We all learn in different ways. Rick learned a lot growing up in Iowa on the farm, playing sports, coaching, working as an athletic director, and officiating high school and college basketball. He's learned on some of the toughest college basketball courts in the United States.

I've had the opportunity to not only watch Rick officiate, and to be on the sideline for games he has officiated, but come to appreciate him as a man. He hasn't been a perfect official, nor a perfect person, because no one is. But what he does demonstrate repeatedly on the court, and in life, and what he and Dave Simon have captured in this book, is that element of imperfection that makes us all human and that can make the team bigger than the sum of its parts.

We all fall down. How we pick up the pieces defines who we are. Rick picks up the pieces when he officiates, and *Whistle in a Haystack* gives the reader multiple lessons of personal growth applicable in our daily lives, in a business environment or in the sports world. That is the beauty of this book, and a reason I'm proud to provide this foreword — because his message is about way more than sports.

If there's anything I'd like the reader to take away from this book, it's that sports give us so much more than just a lesson in who wins or loses. We develop character. We build friendships. We learn the value of being part of a team and how to communicate better. We're taught how to lose with honor. We must figure out how to grow through defeat. And we must come to understand that not everybody is number one, that we all must find our own path.

I've been fortunate enough to win a thousand games and I have lost hundreds of games coaching college basketball. Some hurt badly, and others served to teach important lessons. Regardless of what I took away from the games, I was a better person afterwards, and my team grew from the experience. I hope I shared this with my players, and I hope it is that message that you take away from *Whistle in a Haystack* when you are done reading.

Mike Krzyzewski
Duke Men's Basketball Coach 1980-2015
U.S. Men's Olympic Basketball Coach 2008 and 2012

Preface
A Passion For Officiating and Life

(This essay from Rick Hartzell first appeared in Referee magazine preceding the 2013-2014 college basketball season.)

The people who know how to explain what words mean say that "passion" is a "strong emotion of love or hate, an object of strong desire."

For nearly all of us who are intimately involved in the officiating business, (and it is a business) I think that definition sums up how we feel about our "avocation." I am especially taken by the "love or hate" reference, because it certainly applies. Officiating, like the experiences of life, has so many ups and downs, good nights and bad nights, celebrations and heartbreaks. It seems to me that while many times, for many of us, the "downs" outnumber the "ups," we keep coming back and trying again, because we have a passion for every aspect of this business.

What else would cause us to work all the hours that it takes; to face the daily challenges that confront us to be prepared and competitive; to crawl behind the wheel of a car all hours of the day or night to get to and from games; to spend the precious time that it takes; to work in the cold of the winter and the heat of the summer; to drive six hours one way to a game, in terrible weather, by ourselves, with other of life's issues on our mind; to be paid less than a reasonable wage for really hard work and to be yelled at while doing what few are brave enough to try to do. Passion, that is what causes us to do this; it cannot be anything else.

Long before I was consumed by the officiating bug, I had a

dear friend who told me that "officiating is what I do." As time went on, I came to understood fully what he meant by that statement: If you were going to a) get married, b) have a graduation ceremony or an important family gathering, c) throw a great party, or d) pass away, please do it sometime other than during the basketball season, because if any of these things happen during the season, it is very likely that I won't be there to join you, or at the very least I will be late, and I certainly will be distracted if and when I do get there. That is what passion for something does to a person. Often it skews your judgment of right and wrong, but no one can ever question the passion that officiating brings out in people. Perhaps only people who officiate, their families, friends and peers can really understand it.

Officiating becomes a lifestyle, and cannot be a hobby. That is the way it has to be if you are going to be really good at it, or even just average, for that matter. This business forces you to live and breathe the sport, to have strong emotion for what you are doing, to have "passion" to do the very best you can. You see it in officiating every day, and for the most part, if we use our best judgment, that kind of passion is a healthy thing. For many, that passion is a reason to get up in the morning and work as hard as we do.

By my way of thinking, our priorities should be our faith, our families and our passion for life and its wonderful opportunities, in that order. We cannot let these priorities get out of order, because if they do, we have all sorts of other issues that develop. But if the faith and family parts are solid, then there still is plenty of time for your passion to apply to officiating or other activities. And if officiating is where part of your passion is directed, then you understand exactly what I mean.

I have often thought about why sports officials have this passion for officiating and I think there are many legitimate reasons. Some are: 1) Officiating is very hard to do, no matter what level you choose, or what level chooses you, and that challenge makes it worthwhile. 2) Officiating is full of great people, people who will help and support you, and care about you as a human being whether you work all the big games or not. 3) You can evaluate your work every time you go on the floor. You know how you did, you get immediate and very obvious feedback. 4) The passion you bring to the sport makes it an extremely important part of your life's package.

I was told once that when your regrets outnumber your dreams, then it is time to walk away. Officials have dreams, they believe in themselves and what they are doing, and those dreams make it so you want to get up in the morning and try to do the best you can in order that you can work and compete again. Holding on to those dreams and keeping the passion alive keeps us going day to day, and that is a very good thing. So many people in the world have little to look forward to — they have lost the dream, they do not have the passion, and that is so unfortunate. Sports officials are lucky to have both.

My goal is to live a life of passion every single day. A huge part of that passion for me involves officiating, among a couple of other things. I know that many of you are the same and that we share that bond. If we keep our priorities straight and keep that passion alive, we have everything to live for.

See you in the gym and here is to a passion-filled 2013-14 season. ■

Introduction

Dave Simon and I met 25 years ago. We didn't know a book would come out of that initial relationship.

Since then, I've been blessed to build a highly successful and visible college basketball officiating career, while Simon officiated high school and small college basketball, before leaving the court due to the demands of his full-time job. I would jot down notes throughout the years, capturing ideas and stories — lessons that I felt worth sharing. Dave did the same. I built a huge file. Dave conceptualized ideas.

As we went our own ways over the years, Dave sent a LinkedIn note to me in May 2015 giving some thoughts about a book idea — taking stories from basketball officiating and sharing them so others can gain from the life lessons inherent in the experiences. That stoked me. I had been working on my own book for some time, but could never get it over the hump. So, Dave and I finding each other and reconnecting made this book possible.

Our ensuing conversations led to *Whistle in a Haystack*. Both of us crafted chapters, shaped them, wrote and edited, but it is my stories you'll hear, and my writing with Dave's deft touch, editing and journalistic expertise that guides the effort.

After meeting at a summer basketball officiating camp around 1990, Simon and 1 stayed in touch sporadically over the years, and eventually *Referee Magazine* had Simon do a profile on me. Since then, we have reconnected and joined in our recent efforts to capture life lessons from the hardwood based on my officiating and administrative careers.

Excitement drove our initial conversations. For years, both of us wanted to put together a book based on our officiating experiences, seeing it as a springboard to many lessons that could help others handle tough issues in their lives.

During those conversations, an idea led to a story. A thought led to chapter. A quote created an explanation which generated further discussion.

Simon and I batted around many chapters in early back-and-forth discussions. We settled on those encompassed here. We believe every reader will enjoy reading *Whistle in a Haystack*, and gain from our experiences, including the take-aways at the end of each chapter, which are designed to keep the reader thinking and applying what we've learned on the court.

I have wanted to write a book like this for a very long time. Over years of speaking engagements and interactions with people from all walks of life, it became clear there were many experiences from my basketball officiating, administrative career and some personal life issues that resonated with others. At the grass roots level — particularly people from small towns and Midwestern folks — there is a strong desire to excel and improve their lives and those of the people around them. I am thrilled and honored to work with Dave Simon on this effort and believe we have produced something meaningful and special for others through this book.

"It's been a terrific experience working with Rick because we had similar beliefs about what we've learned officiating basketball. We also both wanted to share these unique stories with others. Over the years, I've said many times that what I learned officiating on the basketball court dwarfs what I've learned in any other facet of my life. You get instantaneous feedback. You have to deal with extremely difficult people. You have to acknowledge you are wrong at times, and move on in a positive way. You improve your communication skills, because if you don't, the next game or play could get worse. Those types of thoughts about being engaged as an official kept me pondering this book for years, and I'm extremely pleased to partner with Rick and get this out for others," Simon said.

We believe you will enjoy this book as much as we had living it on the hardwood court, and writing it. Thanks for joining us on this journey, and we hope you'll share it with others.

[As a side note to readers, there are several terms that will be used interchangeably throughout the book. For sports officials who are purists, using certain generic terms might seem heresy. But for the general reader, we believe the terms will make the book more readable. When we say "sports official," that is the person wearing the striped shirt who makes decisions regarding the rules on the field. His decisions are "rulings," technically speaking, but we will use the term "called," along with other words. You "officiate" a game, but we will use the word "ref" or "worked" at times. The "referee" is the lead official in the game, and in a three-man basketball officiating crew, the other two officials are the umpires. We may call all three "refs" or the "referee" for the casual reader. Again, we apologize in advance to all the rules gurus who read this book, and hope you can roll with the punches on this one.] ◼

Rick Hartzell
Dave Simon

Chapter 1
My First Big Adult Moment

In March of 1989, in my third full year of full-time Division I men's basketball officiating, I caught a break. I worked three rounds of the ACC tournament after 80+ regular season games, and was then selected to officiate the NCAA tournament, where I worked the first weekend.

A phone call followed that I was selected to officiate in the NCAA Regional at the Meadowlands in New Jersey the last weekend of March, a huge step for any college basketball referee at that early stage of their career. I had not given much thought to it — everything in my officiating career had happened quickly. I had a "real" job as Director of Athletics at Bucknell University, and a young family. I focused on hanging in there and making a strong day-to-day effort, not on the big picture — where I might head on the bigger stage of the basketball court.

I was assigned to the Georgetown-North Carolina State game with fellow officials Jim Bain and Tom Lopes.

This was a cool deal — two big name coaches in John Thompson and Jim Valvano and two quality partners in Bain and Lopes.

'Boomer' Bain was a guy who I looked up to and whom everyone regarded as one of the best officials in the country. He was at the end of his long and storied career, so I wanted to do good work with and for him, and Tom. We had a great game—managing the contest well and getting the calls right.

When you work these games, you can tell if you have it going right. The game flows. No one complains. The crowd cheers and focuses on the game, but doesn't boo all the time. The players play, the coaches coach, the officials officiate. On this night we had it all going just right. It was a competitive game, but not necessarily close. Georgetown was the better team, leading by 10 most of the night. N.C. State was the Cinderella team since their magical run to the NCAA title in 1984. Jim Valvano was the charismatic leader of this team that featured stars Rodney Monroe, Tom Gugliatta and Chris Corchiani. I had worked several N.C. State games that season and a couple Georgetown games, so I was familiar with both the players and the coaches. That helped. Late in the game, N.C. State got the game to a six-point deficit. Corchiani started a dribble drive from high on the right wing. I was officiating in the trail position right beside him.

At that moment, my officiating and adult life changed forever — I called a traveling violation on a play where I was splitting hairs, and that is an officiating no-no. Was it a travel? Probably not. Did it have an impact on what officials call 'advantage/disadvantage' for the dribbler? It did not. Could someone in the thirtieth row see that it was a travel? Was it obvious? No it was not. Did it end any chance N.C. State had to win? No, but that is irrelevant. I made a terrible mistake, should have let the play go, and knew it immediately.

Billy Packer, the announcer on CBS, killed me for the call. My partners, whom I let down, were supportive but quiet in the locker room afterwards. My ACC supervisor called me, and even though he was my mentor and this game was not his game (it was NCAA jurisdiction), his words to me were unprintable here. The NCAA representative came in to see us, and in one of the less humane comments ever made, told us that it was unfortunate that call was made because we were ticketed to advance to the Final Four until that happened. Wow...one call, a huge impact, and I could not take it back.

I got in my car for the three-and-a-half hour ride home to Lewisburg, PA. It was 1:30 a.m. I had no one to share my thoughts with on the long ride. My heart hurt, my ego in tatters.

I had missed calls before, every official does; but never one in a game like this. I was alone and hurting. No one had died, but it sure felt like it. I remember getting home, not being able to sleep and going out and just walking around Lewisburg for hours, waiting for the sun to come up. I thought things would be better then. My family did not understand the impact of what I had done. A few of my officiating buddies called me.

They told me, "No big deal, the game was already decided" or "you will be okay, it happens" or "don't worry about it, you were where a million guys would want to be." But, it didn't matter. I knew. I had made a huge mistake. And, somehow I knew that mistake would haunt me for a long, long time. I didn't know that it would have an impact on a 35-year career at that moment, but it did. Some people never forgot.

"He can't close the game" they would say. "The pressure got to him" or "he lost focus at the most important moment" were just a few of the comments I heard.

A lot of guys who officiate have done a lot worse, but this one was about me. It was my burden to carry, my mountain to climb to show everyone that call was not what I was about — I just made a mistake.

A year-and-a-half later, 1 ran into Jim Valvano at the baggage claim of the Raleigh-Durham airport. Valvano was sick at the time, with the cancer that would eventually take his life. I saw him and went over.

I asked how he was and then told him how terribly sorry I was for that call. He was awesome. He laughed, and hugged me and held on to me and squeezed me for just the right amount of time, and he told me not ever to worry about it for a second. He knew what was really important and at that moment — a bad travel call from a game 18 months earlier was trivial in the bigger picture. I am forever thankful for his kind words and perspective.

* * *

An interesting aside to this story happened about a year later. I was the AD at Bucknell at the time and we were working with Georgetown and their long-time assistant coach, Craig Eshrick, to schedule a guarantee game with them in Washington, D.C. We had the game made and were working on a contract, Craig and I, and Craig said, "hey, Coach Thompson wants to talk to you." So, he put Coach Thompson on the phone. What he said really stunned me. Coach Thompson has a very low and strong voice, one that you will never forget once you have heard it. He said, "Rick, I know you have been criticized over that call you made in tournament last March. Let me tell you this. If you had made that call against the big black guy (meaning him) coaching at the other end, instead of that damn Italian at the other end, you would have been a hero. Don't let it bother you in the least. You did a great job and you are a great official. Don't let what stupid people say bother you. See you soon." And, that was it. That call really had an impact on me. And, I never worked a game for Coach Thompson or ever saw him doing radio or television someplace when he didn't give me a huge hug and shake my hand. He is a great man. He had tremendous positive influence on the kids he coached, and he had a huge impact on me. He made me feel okay, over a very hard situation.

* * *

Since then, I have had a long and successful career officiating high-level men's college basketball. Most people have forgotten that call by now, although a few haven't and never will. I understand that — I had a very hard time getting past it for a long while myself. But, I've learned over time that in life you have to move on from the bad stuff. You cannot carry all the burdens or mistakes around forever, or it weighs you down, keeping you from your best performance.

We all need to move forward from our mistakes. How you carry yourself and rebound after those mistakes is really what is important.

Several people have told me that I should have worked multiple Final Four's in my career. I think that one call kept that from happening. It doesn't seem right, but a lot of things aren't right. I decided that I would not let that one bad call define me or define my officiating career. There have been a lot of great calls since (and some clunkers too) but the pain of that night never, ever leaves me completely, regardless of how I process it. ■

Chapter 1 Lessons

1. Life's moments can define us, or we can learn from them. When an incident or event concludes, process it, put it in perspective, then move on. If you carry it with you then paralysis sets in, and you cannot move forward.

2. One moment does not make you who you are. Life is a process, filled with MANY ups and downs for all of us. Accept that we all run into walls, face setbacks and hardship. What makes you a success is getting back up and participating in the game.

3. If you have not challenged yourself then you likely have not failed. You must put yourself in difficult and challenging situations. Doing hard things is good. It makes you grow, it makes you learn, it makes you apply the lessons that you learn, and you often learn those lessons from failure. Keep moving forward.

Chapter 2
You Never Know

Does anything ever turn out the way we imagined or planned it? Things go awry. Circumstances change. People do things we do not expect, and even the best laid plans break down. You never know how things are going to turn out.

Life is filled with ups and downs that are impossible to predict. And, maybe it is best that we don't know exactly how things will go; what fun would that be? It is the challenges of life and the dreams that we have for our lives that keep us going, that get us out of bed each day. When those dreams stop or the learning stops, then a part of us dies.

A friend of mine once told me that when you become a cynic, then you know you are getting old. I try to work as hard as I can to fight those negative thoughts, those thoughts of regret or cynicism, and try to stay young and vibrant and full of dreams of what can yet be accomplished.

It is not an easy era we live in. You get left behind if you don't keep up. With age, you must fight to stay healthy and mobile. As you age in the officiating business, you might have more experience, knowledge, credibility and acceptance, but you don't look as pretty doing the work. That is part of the life cycle.

I try to go by the old adage of the former Negro League baseball pitcher Satchel Paige, who said, "How old would you be if you didn't know how old you was," which is a perfect way to describe the aging process. Birth certificates don't mean much really. How do you feel? What are you doing better? Are some of your dreams alive? Are you challenging yourself with some difficult tasks every day?

In the late 1980s, the ACC (Atlantic Coast Conference), an innovative conference in training and retaining the best men's basketball officiating possible, as well as a league with a deep passion for basketball, ran a series of in-service camps for its officials. Both the veteran officials and the "up and coming" younger officials went to summer camp for in-service work. The older and more experienced officials would instruct and teach, and the younger campers would work games and get valuable critiques and tips on all the issues that came up in games. Camps typically run in July, so the major college head coaches can attend and assess rising high school players. The best players, with the best coaches in attendance, with the best officials teaching, created an atmosphere that demanded quality performance under a high degree of pressure. Officials grew or failed, the cream rising to the top or falling.

One of those camps was held in Princeton, N.J., in 1989. Several high profile ACC veteran officials were there as the instructional staff (Joe Forte, Lenny Wirtz, Dick Paparo, Gerry Donaghy, among others whom I prefer not to name). Those officiating the contests were the next wave of ACC officials, who were being prepared to move up to full time or "referee" status (me, Steve Gordon, Larry Rose, Mike Wood, Duke Edsall, Sam Croft).

We had worked these camps before. The usual drill was work a game, talk to the veteran who watched you, get some feedback, rest, work another game or two and call it a day. Go eat dinner, drink some adult beverages, talk and tell stories, get some rest and then do it again. Pretty low key, not anything out of the ordinary. Try and give your best effort and not screw things up. Then you had a chance to move one more step up a very tall ladder.

We assumed this camp would be like others we'd attended, but soon found out differently. As they say on television, "not so fast my friend." Oh, how this camp would be different.

I and my colleagues found that not only were there more games than usual in this camp, with the best high school players and sponsored by Nike (ABCD Camp), but that there were fewer officials in attendance. It was hot outside, and more so in the gyms. Campers were expected to work five or six games a day in non-air conditioned gyms. Critiques were getting were more personal, degrading, and demeaning.

The boot camp atmosphere was new to each of the campers, who made it through the first day. That night, there was not the usual evening atmosphere of fun and frivolity.

We all knew something was up. They were trying to break us down, to see who could take it and survive the test of will — who could take the personal attacks, who could come back tomorrow and do better, and who would crack and do something stupid or say something they shouldn't and get blackballed forever. Or who would break down physically and just walk — something each of us thought of doing, for sure. But we knew what was going on, because many of these camps do the same thing, to a lesser degree — bring guys in, have them work, tell them how awful they are after the first day, then build them up, teach them, have them do better so they leave feeling good about themselves and the league and the guys that trained them. (And, so they come back again next year, I guess.)

It was torture. We had to endure it, pick each other up, encourage each other to keep going, to stay hydrated to just get through the day. We had no choice but to pass the test if we wanted to do this officiating thing that we all had as our dream. I think they did not understand our level of camaraderie and that at least some of us had some ability to see through what was really going on.

After the camp, the attendees rode to the airport together, unsure if their careers were over before they really had gotten started. No one came unglued. We understood what was going on and we supported each other. We had our butts kicked. We were worn out, physically and mentally. But we bonded. Over 25 years later, we are all still friends. They tried to break us down, but what they really did was make an unbreakable bond.

It's easy to prejudge a situation. But you just never know how it will turn out. Sometimes a bond is created where none existed before. Sometimes basketball officials are ready to take the next jump in their careers. Others fall behind. How we build our house is something that we control.

Never enter into a job, marriage or personal situation thinking that if you do a certain amount of things just right that everything will be okay. Don't expect a situation or relationship to follow a blueprint. Things change. Life is dynamic. You never know what lies ahead.

The unexpected often occurs when we least plan for it. Expect to face some hurdles because everyone does. It is those people who adjust and re-adjust, and who make a decision to overcome hurdles who get the furthest in life.

At the Princeton camp, we made it through a right of passage and showed we had the will to succeed. Sometimes that will is all you have. It keeps you alive, and makes you better, great. ■

Chapter 2 Lessons

1. Things are seldom perfect. We have to adjust, be flexible, change plans in midstream. Re-assess and adjust.

2. Stay engaged. Do not lose your focus even when times get tough. And, stay with it till the end. Then, objectively evaluate and go back at it all over again.

3. "Tough times don't last...tough people do."

Chapter 3
Do What You are Supposed to Do

Wouldn't the world would be a better place if people would just do their jobs? Do what you are supposed to do, what you are hired to do, what your job description says to do, or what you know is the right thing to do.

Think about that for little while. Let it sink in.

Too many people want to tell others how to do their work or job and they don't take care of their own business because they are lazy or just plain unhappy or critical. The perfect example is all the people who go to basketball games just to yell at the referees.

I could tell a million stories of things yelled from the stands — despicable, nasty, personal and inappropriate. It seems that everyone knows how to referee Division I college basketball games. Some people think they know how to do everything that everyone else does. Just do your job, let me do mine. Please.

In the ACC tournament in the early 1990s, I officiated the North Carolina (UNC)-Clemson game with two of my best friends, Steve Gordon of Washington, D.C., and Frank Scagliotta of Pen Argyl, Pennsylvania. We officiated a lot of games together and were (and are) great friends.

Basketball Hall-of-Famer Dean Smith was coaching UNC at the time, and Rick Barnes coached Clemson. Smith was the icon and Barnes the up-and-coming coaching star. Clemson had not beaten UNC often over the years, and there was a toughness Coach Barnes was trying to instill in the Tigers to get them to be able to compete with the Tar Heels and the other ACC powerhouse, Duke.

This was one of the most bizarre incidents in my officiating career, one I remember vividly. Late in the first half, I was in the trail position (the last official coming down the court — hence the term, "trail," for "trailing" the play) in front of the UNC bench. Clemson was on offense.

I overheard Coach Smith, ever the sportsman and the voice of "doing things exactly right," say to a Clemson player "Hey number 15, you are a dirty player." It was clear what was said; I heard the exact words.

Coach Smith was probably right about the player, but it was inappropriate to say what he did during game action. Coach Barnes noticed Smith interacting with his player, and the chaos was on. He charged toward the scorer's table and demanded we stop the game. As Clemson scored and the ball went in the basket, I hit the whistle and stopped the clock. I walked toward Barnes to try and calm him down, and Steve Gordon went immediately to Coach Smith to do the same. At that moment there was no calming down Rick Barnes. He was ready to go.

Scagliotta or 'Scags' as we fondly call him, was the referee in the game, so he came to me and asked what was going on. I briefly explained that Coach Smith said something to a Clemson player and that Coach Barnes was incensed about it and came to the table. Frank, composed as always, said, 'Well, let's bring the two coaches together at the scorer's table and we will sort this out.'

That seemed like a good idea at the time, so that is what we did.

Gordon got Coach Smith and I got Coach Barnes and we met at the table—three officials, two head coaches. No one else could hear what was going on.

When we got to the table and before anything else was said, Coach Barnes pointed at Dean Smith and said, "Coach Smith, I am going to kick your ass, right here, right now."

Wow. There were a couple of seconds of silence because none of us could ever believe that anyone would speak to Coach Smith that way, and then Scags, as only he could, said, "Well, I guess bringing them together to talk wasn't such a great idea, huh?" And, fortunately that broke the tension.

That simple comment made all five participants — coaches and officials — realize that we were in the middle of something that had to be calmed down and returned to normalcy. The game was on national TV, and the five of us were in front of a packed house at the Charlotte Coliseum. We had to do what was right.

I took Coach Smith and Gordon took Coach Barnes and ushered them back to their benches so the game could resume.

When I got Coach Smith back to his bench, he looked up at me and said, "Rick, you aren't going to leave me just yet, are you?" I thought for a second and said, "No Coach, I won't leave you right away, but if you think I am going to fight Coach Barnes for you, then you are wrong." Smith smiled.

In a few seconds, I, Gordon and Scags put the ball in play and got back to doing what we were there to do, officiate the game, make the calls, work with and for the coaches and try to get the game right.

After the game, which I believe UNC won, we were all called to a big pow-wow with the ACC Commissioner, Gene Corrigan, our supervisor, Fred Barakat, and the two coaches. We were all called to the principal's office for a discussion.

We three partners described what happened. The commissioner and Barakat met with the coaches. It was a tense, difficult, uncomfortable situation. But it was all defused by Scagliotta's innocent comment, which broke the tension. The coaches got their wrists slapped.

And, the three of us, believe it or not, got commended. We got applauded, got props, for doing just what we should have done. We did what our job description asked of us. We officiated the game and we worked with the coaches and we defused a tense and difficult situation that could have gotten a lot worse. We stayed calm in the face of chaos. That was our job.

There are many "what-ifs" in life, too. What if Barnes had punched Coach Smith? What if the situation had escalated or Scagliotta hadn't said the perfect thing? We'll never know.

What we do know is that doing your job, staying on top of things and executing make for a better outcome for everyone. It doesn't matter if you are a basketball coach, sports official or the guy working the line at General Motors making sure the bolt goes properly on the tire. Do your job, do it right, and the world is a better place.

And we told the truth and worked together. We reacted well and calmly amidst the chaos of a highly charged, competitive situation. We took care of business just the way we were supposed to. That's a huge signal of a job well done. ■

Chapter 3 Lessons

1. Take care of your own business, and work hard at it. If you do that and if you do your work at a high level, then you will be rewarded appropriately.

2. Let others take care of their own business. Keep your eye on your prize, don't interfere and don't try to fix what you can't or shouldn't.

3. When everyone handles their end of the situation, everyone benefits. Do what you are supposed to do, what you are trained to do, what you job description entails.

4. Don't expect to get told how great you do when all you do is meet the expectations that have been set forth.

Chapter 4
The Journey

I compare life to a bike ride up a hill. Sometimes, the hill is steep, the wind is behind you and the road is paved and the riding easy. But, invariably, the riding gets harder, there are obstacles in the road and you have to slow down or even stop on your trip up that hill. You may even slide back down the hill or have to go around an obstacle in order to continue to make progress going up that hill.

You want to get to the top, because the expectation is that things will be easier once you arrive — it's all downhill from there. But it's not easy to get to the top. If it were easy to get to the top, would it be worth anything once you got there? The struggle makes it sweeter.

"If it were easy, everyone would do it" was a line my dad used to drop on me. That ride up the hill will be filled with potholes. Sometimes you can pedal harder and make it up the hill. Sometimes you have to stop and catch your breath and regroup. It is never completely smooth sailing. Things happen.

Enjoy the happy times, challenge yourself to meet the harder times head-on, and with an optimistic attitude while you pedal, you can make it to the top. The great coach, Jim Valvano, who was featured in Chapter One, said it best, "Don't give up, don't ever give up'."

There's a phrase in the officiating business, "You're only as good as your last call or your last game." You cannot rest on what you have accomplished or you will quickly slide back down that hill. There are no days off when you can coast or take it easy. You have to pedal hard, work hard, give your best effort on that day. I always try to referee with one thing in mind: Every game is important to someone.

If you look at games that way, work them for 40 minutes with the best you have to give on that night, then you will keep climbing that hill. And, you won't slide back. The game, coaches, kids, fans and families deserve that.

I have always been bothered by a few officials who were more worried about where they were going next or their next trip than they were about today's game. Today's game has to be the most important thing to you. If you continue to concern yourself with tomorrow's game or next week's game or the championship game, then pretty soon today's game is gone, and if you aren't good in today's game then tomorrow's game might not ever come around again.

At this stage of my career, I make it a point every single night to savor what is going on around me. I enjoy the pregame time in the locker room with my fellow officials — getting caught up, talking about the game at hand, new rules, recent experiences, how the family is doing.

I savor the *National Anthem* and use that time to say "thanks" for how lucky I am to have been a part of the game for the 4,000 + other college basketball games I've officiated. I lose myself in the moment. Invariably, at those times, I think about my dad, Bob, who showed me his love for sports at an early age. My dad never got to see me play or officiate at a high level. He would have been so proud of me.

That wasn't the case earlier in my career. My mental focus wasn't as strong. My mind strayed. I wasn't engaged. I knew that had to change.

To be a great sports official, or to be successful at any other endeavor that takes intense focus, you must lose yourself in your work to the point where you have nothing else impacting your thought process. I compare that moment to the time you spend watching a great movie; you are lost in the moment, you forget about everything else.

The best guys and gals can get in that game and be so focused that they do not miss anything going on. They are locked-in, rock solid, on top of it all. That does not mean they don't miss a call or a play now and then. That will happen. But it didn't happen because of a lack of focus or attention. They weren't slipping back down the hill; they were pedaling hard.

A couple of years ago, I worked the West Virginia-Kansas game at Allen Fieldhouse in Lawrence, Kansas. The arena was loud, rocking, chaotic — a great college basketball atmosphere.

Kansas is one of the best places to work, in my opinion. Those environments force you to be at your best or you will get exposed. I was standing in my time-out spot in that game with Coach Bob Huggins of West Virginia (he's an all-time great guy as a college coach, someone I always enjoyed working for — a 'man's man'). He was mad at me for what he thought was a weak post foul. He screamed at me during a time out.

At the other end, Coach Bill Self of Kansas was mad about an illegal screen that I called a few plays before. So he is yelling down the court at me. The band is playing and the cheerleaders are doing their flips and cheers. Fans are screaming and carrying on, and there I stand — hands behind my back, chin up, relaxed, calm, motionless, and for the most part emotionless — the way you have to be to do a great job in this crazy business. You must keep your composure while everyone around you is losing theirs. You cannot show that any of the craziness going on around you has an impact on you. You must exhibit a calm demeanor. Over time, that demeanor builds a perception of trust, and trust is the great official's calling card.

I found my moment. I took it all in — the bad and the good. I knew right then that every step in the game is there to be appreciated, like life situations. My journey was on that court — getting chewed out and screamed at, accepting what was coming my way as part of the game and the profession I'd chosen.

I often get asked why I officiate. My answer is always the same, "Because it is really hard to do." I am paid reasonably well and get satisfaction from doing a good job, but it's more than that. The satisfaction comes from doing something that most people could not do, something that is very hard, almost impossible sometimes.

The satisfaction from officiating comes from doing something that you know is very hard. You must stay calm, get the plays right and be professional with coaches, players and everyone else involved with the game. It is hard to describe walking out of the tunnel at some of these — everyone going crazy, and you have to be calm, collected and sure of yourself so when others lose their minds and objectivity, you don't.

Not only do you have to get the plays right, but you must control the chaos, do the baby sitting with coaches and players. Basketball officials have to manage the scorekeepers and timers at the table. They must tune out the fans and be in "the zone" in terms of concentration. They must consistently have 95% + accuracy in their calls and judgment. And at the Division I level, they operate under the highest level of scrutiny.

It is hard. Sometimes downright impossible. And, that is what makes it fun. Everyone should find something in their life that is really hard to do. Maybe it is a hobby, or running a half marathon, or rebuilding a car, or putting an addition on the house, or learning to cook. What you choose is not the most important thing. Doing something to challenge yourself and stretch yourself and to accomplish something you thought might be out of your reach is important. Stretch. Reach. Pedal hard. Get way outside your comfort zone. You can get to the top of that hill! ■

Chapter 4 Lessons

1. Learn from each moment along your journey. Your journey will be more difficult (at times) than you could ever have imagined. Accept the tough times, along with the good. Use those moments for perspective.

2. Great people are just ordinary people with an extraordinary amount of determination.

3. Remember these truths about your journey:

   a) Doing what you want to do will be different than you imagined it would be.

   b) It will be more difficult than you imagined it would be.

   c) It will be better than you ever imagined it would be. When you reach a personal peak, savor it. You are reaching your potential. Share what you know with others — it doesn't get any better than that.

Chapter 5
A Moment's Joy

As we move through life, it is important to find some time for happiness, for joy. That's what I would term, "put aside" or "set aside" joy, because it doesn't just happen. You have to make time for it.

Life is filled with trials and tribulations for all of us, and even though we look around and see people whom we think have it made, we do not walk in their shoes. No one escapes the issues life presents. Each of us needs to have things to look forward to and each of us needs some joy and happiness in order to live a life that is full and rewarding.

I often go to the local public library to think and write. On some days, a large group of mentally challenged adults come into the library, often in the area where I sit. They are friendly and polite and very considerate of trying to be quiet while they read magazines or just sit and relax. Several things about the group amaze me.

First, I refuse to get up and move when they come in. I do not want to make a single one of them feel bad. Second, if I pick up something that they drop or if I help them in any small way, they are so thankful. And third, they find joy in the smallest things, things that each of us just take for granted. They have joy, something that comes in different ways to all of us.

One night in the early 1990s, I was officiating a game in State College, Pennsylvania. I had worked at Penn State many times prior to the university joining the Big 10. They were happy to have me. The facilities and the people were good, and the fans, though small in number, were always gentle and friendly.

On this night, they were playing Brigham Young in a non-conference game. Brigham Young had a good team, as usual, and they were leading Penn State by double figures. I had officiated BYU several times and had a good relationship with their coach. Late in the game, with the win secured, the coach called me over and said, "Rick, do you see the older gray-haired lady there behind the bench? Number 10 on the end of my bench is her grandson and she has never seen him play. I am going to put him in with under a minute to play. He's not very good, but she has never seen him play and if you get a chance can you try and get him to the free throw line to see if he can score? He will never score from the field."

I have a soft spot in my heart for kids who work hard and don't get to play — maybe because I was one of them in my football career at the University of Northern Iowa. So, I said to the coach, "Sure Coach, I will see what I can do."

Number 10 came into the game and the coach winked at me. The game was over, BYU leading by 20 with under a minute, and sure enough, number 10 drove with the ball down the lane, got bumped a little and I ruled a foul.

It was a foul I would not have called if the game was in question. I never messed with the integrity of games, but this time was different. The game was decided. The gray-haired, aging grandmother had never seen her grandson play, much less score. So, I put him on the line for a one-and-one free throw. He made the first shot and from my position across the court, the BYU coach yelled at me to get my attention.

I looked over to the head coach, and he said, "Hey Rick, just kidding."

The lady behind the bench was not his grandmother — the coach got me. He wanted the kid in the game and to get to the line, and he duped me. Little did he know all he would have had to do was ask and I would have done it anyway, having done so previously for Bo Ryan's (University of Wisconsin Men's Head Basketball Coach) son at the University of Wisconsin-Milwaukee, when Bo came to watch him play under the same circumstances.

I felt good about both instances because I had done something to give a young man (not the fake grandmother in this case) some real joy. He scored in a Division I basketball game and all his hard work paid off. This might have been the greatest moment of his life, something he could tell his kids when he was a dad or grandfather and it did not hurt anyone. We should try to live life this way — appreciate the joy of each key moment.

Another night in that same season, I was working a Big East game at St. John's University in New York City, with an excellent, veteran official named Larry Lembo. Larry was one of the original guys who officiated a lot of games in the Big East as it developed into a major force in college basketball. Larry was a great guy, a dad, a grandpa, big and strong, with a powerful presence on and off the court.

Near the end of this game, with the outcome decided, a player off the bench for the visiting team caught a long pass well behind the St. John's defense. He took about six steps with the ball and then dunked it.

Lembo was the official nearest to the play. I was coming up the court and watched it develop, looked at Lembo and thought, "If he isn't going to call that, then neither am I."

It is an unwritten rule of basketball officiating that you almost never come out of your primary area of responsibility to make a call in front of an accomplished partner unless it is to save a close game where a call just has to be made. Lembo was an accomplished official and this was not a game-saver situation, so I did not blow the whistle.

When we got into the locker room, we sat down for a post-game discussion of plays and issues that occurred. As we wrapped it up, I asked Larry, "Can you tell me why you let that open court travel go there at the end of the game?"

Larry looked at me and said, "Rick, that kid may never ever get a chance to do that again. Who am I to take that joy away from him?"

I never forgot that comment. The travel was irrelevant. The game was long ago decided. And Larry Lembo, the gentleman, let a kid have a moment of joy that he will never forget. Lesson learned.

It is important for us all to understand and recognize the moments of joy that occur right in front of us every single day. Give a little joy to someone when you have that opportunity. We need to not only hand these to others, but also embrace them for ourselves, and savor them.

Joy is fleeting. It is not a given. Times can get tough, life can be difficult. Enjoy the joyous moments that you have or that you give. Both reward you. ■

Chapter 5 Lessons

1. Experience and savor the moments of joy. Don't ever let anyone steal your joy from you.

2. Share with others the joy that life brings. Celebrate that joy. Then, go back to work and create some more.

3. It may only seem like a little thing, but if you can shine the spotlight on someone else, it might just be one of the defining moments of his or her life. Never underestimate the power of a positive experience or a positive word to someone. You might be the spark that ignites something great

Chapter 6
Beyond Preparation

There are many reasons why some people are successful while others aren't, regardless of their chosen field or their relationships. Talent sets some people apart. Other times it is luck, good fortune or great timing. Some people are just more organized or they mature more quickly or they get the right education, the right break at an opportune moment. Preparation separates others from the pack.

I have met a huge number of great people in my life, including some of the brightest and best in college administration, sports, and officiating. Many of them have been and are extraordinarily bright, charismatic or talented — a cut above.

Preparation set those individuals apart. They were not surprised at what happened to them or for them. They took advantage of situations that occurred because they were ready.

Leonard ("Lenny") Wirtz was one of those individuals, one of my teachers when it came to high-level college basketball. Lenny was not tall — standing 5'5" — nor big in physical stature. But he had an overwhelming positive presence and was the epitome of what it means to be prepared. One could argue he was obsessively prepared.

In my second year on the ACC officiating roster, I was assigned to 30 games with Wirtz as his referee (the head official in a three-man crew). I was almost always assigned in the Umpire 1 position, and the third official changed almost every night, as is the custom. I knew what was going on.

Fred Barakat, our outstanding supervisor, was testing me. He knew Lenny would not let a game get out of control. Fred was giving me an opportunity to succeed, and Lenny was either going to train me or he was going to tell Mr. Barakat to get rid of me — sink or swim, with Lenny as my instructor, leader, mentor.

After our first game together, Lenny said to me, "Kid, if you will just shut up and listen and do what I teach you, I think you might have a chance to be pretty good some day." I never forgot those words. Be quiet, do your job, and don't do anything to mess up the game. Let Lenny take the hard plays and deal with the coaches. Do your part, but don't try to be a hero.

At that time in the ACC, well before other conferences began doing it, there was an extremely high level of game-by-game scrutiny on officials that included a referee's game report, a supervisor who reviewed the tape of every game and made a report, and at least one if not two observers at every game who filed a report. Every game was on TV, so there was always scrutiny. You were either good enough or you were gone.

Lenny Wirtz lived by the 6P principle: Perfect Preparation Prevents Piss-Poor Performance. I heard him say it many times.

If you worked a game with Lenny, you knew that 45 minutes before you went on the court there would be a comprehensive pregame conference. If you worked five games in five days, you would have that very same pregame conference every single game. I probably worked 100 games with Lenny over my career, and we had the exact same pregame every single game. It never varied. I could repeat it verbatim right now. You were prepared for every single possible event that Lenny had ever encountered in his illustrious career.

In one of my first games with Lenny, we were at North Carolina State. I'll never forget it. They were playing Morgan State out of Baltimore. During the game, a couple of players got to trash talking each other and one of the Morgan State players called one of the N.C. State players an obscenity. I blew the whistle and called a technical foul. Within five seconds, Lenny was right in front of me. "What do you have? Where was the ball? Was there contact? Which end are you going to shoot at? What kind of a technical foul is it? Where will the ball be put in play after the shots are taken?" Lenny rattled those questions off. I was stunned.

I replied to Wirtz, "I don't know the answers to any of those questions. What I know is that number 24 cursed at number 12." The lesson from the great Lenny Wirtz was obvious to me: Be prepared. When you call a technical foul, know exactly what will happen next. Do not mess this up, do it right, by the book, every time. If you are prepared enough you will know exactly what to do when you have made a call like this. If you are not prepared you will mess it up. Not satisfactory.

At the Five-Star Camp in Pittsburgh, where the ACC provided camp supervisors to help teach younger officials, Fred Barakat stood up after lunch and addressed the group. Afterwards, he mentioned that later in the evening, the camp counselors and college players were going to play a camp counselor game. He wanted Wirtz to pick two of the current staff officials to work that game while the rest of the officiating counselors sat with the younger officials to point out what was being done and why.

Wirtz chose Bob Donato and me to work the game with him. Wirtz called me and Donato together and said, matter-of-factly, "We will have a pregame in my room tonight at 6 p.m."

Now, mind you, this was July. This was a summer camp game that did not matter to anyone. It was going to be played at 10:30 p.m. in front of 100 referee campers. But, Lenny Wirtz was not going to be unprepared or embarrassed. He was a professional and he was going to be absolutely certain that the product he put on the floor was the best he could give. July, November or March in the Final Four, it did not matter.

I worked my first Duke vs. North Carolina game in 1993. Annually, it is one of the biggest college basketball games of the year, regardless of the teams' records. Both teams have great coaches, reputations and highly recruited players on their rosters. My partners were Wirtz and Dick Paparo — two of the best officials in the country at the time.

Lenny gave us strict instructions to meet him outside room 117 at the Triangle Hotel at the Raleigh-Durham Airport at 5 p.m. for the short ride over to Cameron Indoor Stadium. I was there at 4:55 with my bag in the car and sitting in my appointed spot, back seat, passenger side of the compact rental car; 5 p.m. came. Lenny was sitting in the driver's seat. He looked at his watch. He put the car in drive and left the hotel without Paparo. I said to Lenny, "Hey Lenny, don't you think we ought to wait for Dick?'"

"Nope," Wirtz replied. "It's five o'clock. I said we were leaving at five. He's a big boy; he will get there. We are doing our pregame at 5:45 with or without him. You and I will be prepared for this game."

True story. That was Lenny Wirtz. Prepared, beyond reproach. There was no wiggle room with Lenny. Issues were black and white, cut and dried, his way or the highway, every time, no variations.

Later in my career, I said to my partners when I was the referee on the game, "Let's not let anything happen that surprises us."

Surprises kill you as an official. If something happens and you do not know what to do or how to react or what ruling to make, you are in big trouble. And sometimes things happen that you have never seen before. If you know the rules and are prepared (6P's), then you have a chance of sorting things out and not being embarrassed.

When the great Chris Collins played at Duke, his teammates would set low post and baseline screens for Chris, in order to get him open. I was working a Duke game one night when they set all sorts of these screens. Chris came to the baseline, rubbed his defender off the screens and then ran the defender into the basket standard, which was out of bounds under the basket. He grabbed the edge of the standard and propelled himself in bounds and caught the ball for a quick jump shot. I knew the play did not look right. I knew he gained an advantage. I knew he could not be the first to touch the ball when he came in from out of bounds. I made the call. I was right. Thank you, Lenny.

Another night, Oklahoma played Coppin State, which had a well-known character for their head coach, Ron 'Fang' Mitchell. Fang was a great guy. At one point in the game, an Oklahoma player stole the ball and went down court all alone for a dunk. When he went up to dunk the ball, it went through the rim, hit his shoulder and bounded straight back up and back through the rim out to the free throw line, where a Coppin State player caught the ball and proceeded to walk out of bounds with the ball, thinking the dunk counted and was worth two points.

I knew the rule. The basket only counts if the ball clears the net. No basket. But, the Coppin State player traveled when he caught the live ball. I had the good fortune of going over to Fang to explain the play. We had a good laugh. I was prepared.

So it goes in refereeing or in life. Don't be surprised. Be prepared to react to all scenarios. Expect the unexpected. With extra preparation, you have a great chance at being successful. ∎

Chapter 6 Lessons

1. The 6P Theory (Perfect Preparation Prevents Piss-Poor Performance) works.

2. Minimize opportunities that could surprise (and hurt) you. Consider multiple options and be ready to apply them at a moment's notice regardless of your situation.

3. Learn from the best — people who have great experience at doing things the right way and apply what they know and have taught you.

Chapter 7
Finish What You Start

"Resolve" is a tremendous trait. Along with "will," resolve takes you a long way in life. Being resolute means doing everything you can to be successful. You don't back down. You do exactly what you are supposed to do in every possible situation. As a sports official, you enforce the rules and don't let anything deter you from doing what is right. You "enforce or you enable."

Many basketball coaches play hard man-to-man, in-your-face defense. They try to have their players stretch the rules by holding, chucking, pushing, grabbing or getting any defensive advantage that they can by using physical play that goes past the acceptable level of play.

Rick Pitino, the outstanding coach of Kentucky, the Boston Celtics and now the Louisville Cardinals, often said his team was going to try and "out-foul the referees" in games. That means he wanted his teams to play physically (not dirty) and see how many fouls the referees would call before they got tired of blowing the whistle.

Referees are human beings (surprise!) and they know when the game has turned into a march to the foul line. They know fans hate that kind of basketball. They know that if there are 70 fouls called in a game and 85 free throws shot, that the game will not be aesthetically pleasing to watch. They know that with every foul call, someone will complain that they are calling too many. Another fan will yell that too few fouls have been whistled. You can't win.

A supervisor might not like when a lot of fouls are called and the rules strictly enforced, and the TV people hate it.

But you have to have resolve. If you stop blowing your whistle, you are not doing your job, and you let the players and the coach determine the style played that night. That style can often be to their advantage and to the disadvantage of the other team. The game is not fair. Both teams do not have an equal chance to win, and as an official that is your only job. Give both teams a chance to win.

I officiated a Clemson-North Carolina game in the early 1990s. At that point in time, and to this day, Clemson has never beaten North Carolina at Chapel Hill — an incredible sports statistic. Rick Barnes was the coach at Clemson, and convinced that the reason Clemson could not beat North Carolina was because his teams backed down when they played the Tar Heels.

They played too soft. Barnes was going to change that mindset. I worked the game with Sam Croft and Steve Gordon. We knew the game would be difficult, they all were. But this was the most unusual game you could imagine. Clemson started fouling North Carolina at the start of the game and never stopped. The outcome of this game was never in question. Clemson wanted to make a statement; they were not concerned about the final score. They played so physically that we had no choice but to blow the whistle, call the fouls and never stop. If we did stop, a scuffle or a fight could easily have occurred.

The game was hand-to-hand combat, with over 75 fouls in the game (30 is about average). Clemson started with 12 players and by the 4:00 mark of the second half they only had five players left. Seven had fouled out. That's 35 fouls. Five guys left on the floor had three or four fouls each. Clemson had over 50 fouls in the game, and eventually only four players left to play.

Every time a player fouls out in any game, one of the officials goes to the coach to notify him of the foul-out and asks him to get another player in the game. At that time, the coach has 30 seconds to respond and put a player on the court. I was the guy in the box.

I had a decent professional relationship with Coach Barnes. So, on every foul out, I went to him, informed him of what the situation was and asked for a substitute. On each occasion, the comments or eye-roll or body language got worse and worse. Finally, when one of the five players remaining fouled out and I went to tell Rick, he looked at me and said, "What do you want me to do now, I don't have anyone left?" It wasn't the time for a remark that wasn't 100 percent professional in nature even though the thought came to my mind. I said, "Rick, that is not my problem. You can play with four. But if you don't stop fouling sometime, there won't be anyone left to play, and you will need at least two players to get the ball in bounds."

Barnes knew that, and responded to me, "And we are not going to stop fouling, so you will just have to keep calling them then."

Fortunately the game was near the end, because Clemson did not stop. We did our job and were resolute. We set the standard for the game. We drew a line in the sand and stood by it. We did what we were supposed to do, and blew the whistle. It was not fun. It was not pretty. But we had no choice.

On the basketball court, a sports field, your job or in life, see things through to the end. You can't stop halfway. Stay on top of the game or your job. People and unusual situations can derail you if you let them.

I know a job well done is one that is seen through to the end. Seeing things through yields a sense of accomplishment and demonstrates resolve and a willingness to do whatever is necessary without giving in. Finishing what you start stretches your personal and professional boundaries. It's a lesson I see repeatedly on the basketball court, and one I know applies in all our daily lives. ■

Chapter 7 Lessons

1. Be resolute. Do not get weak when you know what is right to do. Apply the rules to the situation at hand.

2. There are times in your life when you cannot back down. Plant your feet and stand on principle, and do what you know is right to do. It is not easy. But you can look yourself in the mirror when you do this.

3. Finish what you start. Do not change the rules midstream or it confuses the boundaries for others.

Chapter 8
Be a Great Partner

There are many opportunities for us to be good partners in our lives. Certainly, in our marriages or our "significant other" relationships, being a good and strong partner is crucial to the success of the relationship. There are many other life opportunities for us to show great partnering — in our workplaces, in our social circles, church or community groups. Many of us have workout partners who push us to do more and better in our regular fitness routines. The necessary qualities for being a great partner are similar in all these situations. Here I've listed several common qualities for a great partner:

- A great partner protects your back. S/he stands beside you, defends you, stands up for you and you can count on that person when the going gets tough.
- A great partner supports you and helps to make you better without wanting or looking for credit. A great partner wants nothing from supporting you for themselves; but they want to enhance what you are doing, or make your life better.

- A great partner only cares about getting things right. "It's not who is right, it is what is right." And, getting it right is what is most important.
- A great partner helps you in any way possible.

There is nothing more important in the officiating business than a great partner. (Or, two great partners when you work in a three-person crew.) In almost every game, a situation comes up where two or all three of the officials must come together to figure out something crucial to the flow or outcome. That goes for every sport where officiating comes into play. It might be a clock situation, a rule interpretation, the application of a rule, or a judgment; a variety of situations require a great partner to help figure things out.

There are hundreds of examples of these types of situations that have arisen in my career, and inevitably my partner or partners have come through to help me, or I have come through to help them manage a difficult situation. Sometimes it's no more than a word or two, a simple confirmation of what they thought had happened or how they planned to rule on a play. Other times, that help is much more — significant input or enough information to change someone's mind or interpretation in order to 'save the game' in officiating parlance.

I have many great friends in the officiating business. One such friend is Steve Olson. We started officiating together in the Big 10, and became close friends over the years. Olson and I have similar backgrounds and upbringings — raised on farms in rural Iowa and Wisconsin, respectively, sharing the same beliefs and values. We have strong family ties and are big ex-athletes who found officiating as a way to give back and to serve as a second career. We worked full-time jobs in our primary careers, along with a full basketball officiating schedule. And, both loved our families, wives, kids, and making that our focus in life. I worked a lot of games with "Oly" over the years, some easy, some hard. Some were higher profile games, others less so.

We were chosen to work the Conference USA Championship game together one day in March in the mid-2000s. It was Louisville vs. Memphis, in Memphis. Great coaches — Rick Pitino vs. John Calipari. A lot was on the line. Memphis was rated in the Top 10 in the country. CBS television was there.

We worked our tails off as a crew, and had a great game in what was a nip-and-tuck, close and highly competitive game. I had to make calls on about six straight plays late in the game. That is how it goes some nights. Sometimes you don't have any plays in your lap (or primary area) and some nights you get them all. It is unexplainable. In this case, we were getting plays right, along with the ones I had down the stretch.

With about 15 seconds to go in the game, I called a foul against Memphis, which put a Louisville player on the line for two shots, in a tie game on a play where the defender hit the offensive player in the head on a layup shot. Of course, the boos rang down, but I knew it was the correct call — I had a great look and the right angle. The Louisville player made two, so Louisville led by two points. We came down the court on the last possession by Memphis, with heightened awareness of the situation. We did not want to miss a play now.

Fate intervened. Right between Oly and me, the Memphis point guard took a three-point jump shot and he was fouled.

It was a clear foul. We both called the play, Oly from the trail position in front of the Memphis bench, and me from the center, across the court. We made eye contact, and Oly gave me an imperceptible nod indicating that I should take the play. He did not have to do this. Either one of us could have taken it, and easily it could have been him. But, he knew that I had called the prior play against Memphis. This one was for them. He knew if I took it, I would be off the hook, the game was balanced, no one would hold me responsible for anything that took place in terms of who won and who lost. He was being the true great partner at just the right time. I would not have thought less of him one bit if he had taken the play. Most importantly, we got the play right, which made the moment that much sweeter.

The Memphis player hit the first free throw, missed the next two, and Louisville won by a point. Crazy finish. Fun game. And, my partner made me look like a champ.

In life or on the basketball court, there are times you need a tough partner, one who will tell you what you don't necessarily want to hear. Sometimes you need a good listener or someone who gives great emotional support. Other times you need some-one who gets it and understands situations and human dynamics and balance. The best partners in any part of life have chem-istry. They play off each other. They capitalize on each other's strengths. The key is finding the right partner.

I worked over a hundred games with one of the best referees of his era, Ed Hightower. Ed was very visible and successful on the court, and an excellent school administrator.

In addition to being an outstanding basketball official, Ed was a great dad and husband. I loved to work with Ed because he was a great partner — he knew his strengths and weaknesses and was great with coaches and players. If they ever got out of line, Ed took care of it. He would talk, he would coerce, he would admonish if necessary. But you never had to worry about game management with Ed. He took care of it. All you had to do was call your plays, get them right, stay out of the way, and let Ed do the rest. A great partner, every time. There is nothing better.

Great partners don't come along every day. Partnerships take time to develop and blossom. When they do, the individuals bond. You support each other on the way up and more importantly, when you are down. That's where both earn their stripes. You trust each other implicitly and speak openly.

Oly and Ed are two of the greatest partners anyone could have while officiating basketball. I've been fortunate to officiate so many games with both, and they've enriched my life on and off the court. ■

Chapter 8 Lessons

1. Being a great partner, in any facet of life, is one of the most important things we can do for others. The acts of being a great partner impact others continuously in a positive vein, and will never be forgotten by those affected by that support.

2. Unyielding support of your partner is crucial to long-term success of any relationship — in business, the workplace, on a team or as a sports official.

3. Put yourself second and your partner first — that gives the greatest satisfaction and makes you a terrific partner.

Chapter 9
Perception

There is truth to the adage, "perception is reality." People make decisions based on their perceptions. Take politics — few people take an in-depth look at Presidential candidates, for example. They get a perception of what someone is like or what they believe in, their values, from a sound bite or a snippet from an interview, or from a picture of the candidate hugging a baby or an elderly citizen. That perception is only a snapshot of the bigger picture.

It is not any different in basketball officiating. If you have trust, longevity and believability, then others perceive you are a good basketball referee. Being perceived as topnotch comes from being around for a long time, working a lot of games and being on television frequently. Fans, players and coaches assume you must be really good or you wouldn't be assigned high visibility games.

Coaches also see officials at summer camps working with younger officials and that strengthens how others perceive you. A strong positive perception gives you a greater margin for error to survive a bad call or a bad game or big mistake because others see you as fair, honest, hard-working and in the top percentile of college basketball officials. It takes a long time to build a positive perception.

It feels like it takes forever. You have to build that reputation/perception one game at a time. In fact, it comes in four-minute segments at a time, one half at a time, one game at a time. And, you have to do it over and over and over, night after night, season after season, decade after decade. You must get people to believe in you. If they do, you can almost do no wrong. If they don't, you can do no right. I have witnessed this phenomenon time after time. Two officials can make the identical call. One will go unchallenged (by the veteran or accepted guy) and the other will get abused — simply because he isn't trusted yet or has not been visible enough to develop the respect that leads to trust.

The officiating business is a physical and mental undertaking. You have to learn through your experiences, many of them negative in nature. You learn, grow, develop and mature.

After you reach the stage where you have credibility and trust, and the perception of you is that you are really, really good, then, all of a sudden, you can't run as well as you need to. You are better in every way, except you are not as pretty. Like the aging actress, your parts (assignments) are not as good or frequent. Your visibility is reduced. Your NCAA assignments and conference tournament assignments dwindle or go away.

I consider the last 10-15 years of my officiating life my best.

They have been my most successful years. I finally conquered the credibility and perception part. People know I have been around, worked 3,500 games, many of them the big ones. I am not as pretty as I once was, but coaches know me by name, like they do other top officials.

Great officials, such as Jim Burr, Tim Higgins, Joey Crawford, Danny Crawford and many others, were perceived at the top of their profession because of a specific constant: They were seen as being able to do the job better than others. It is all about perception. Many times perception is reality.

They will do it their way, but they will do it right. They do not care who wins the game. People cut them some slack and let them do their job and that makes them even better.

How you look is important at work, in your personal life, and as a basketball official both on and off the court.

You have to look the part. You have to be in shape and athletic looking. You need to carry yourself with confidence, have a presence that tells people you are in charge but not arrogant, that you know you are good but not overwhelmed by your own ego. A supervisor a long time ago told me something I will never forget: 'Be firm but friendly.' That adage is perfect. Coaches and players will respond to strength and discipline, but the way that message is communicated is much more important than the message itself.

The successful basketball officials from the past few decades almost always have the total package. They look the part. They are strong in nature and in physical attributes. They are confident but not over-bearing. There are exceptions, like Tim Higgins, one of college basketball's all-time best.

He was short, round and not-so-athletic-looking. But he was great, and everyone knew it. He communicated exceptionally well, and knew exactly when the game needed a whistle. And, he communicated bad news better than anyone I knew.

Mike Wood, a dear friend of mine from our years of officiating basketball together, never got the credit he deserved. He didn't look very athletic. But he was a great play caller — one of the very best in my opinion. There were no phantom calls with Mike. If he called it, it happened — a great trait to have. Wood was one of the best officials of my era not to make the Final Four.

Wood, Steve Welmer and me, I have heard a lot of people say. They should have gone.

Coaches don't care where an official stands or what his mechanics look like. They care about your focus on the game, that you are fully engaged and involved, and that you treat them and their players fairly and firmly with dignity and respect. Coaches want you to break a sweat and work hard, to bring your best every night.

If you are on television one night and then the next night you go to another gym to work a game, the first thing the coach wants to know is if you are going to work as hard on his game which is not televised as you did the night before when the stage was bigger and the lights brighter. That was always the night I tried to work even harder. I never wanted anyone to think that I was not giving my maximum effort.

If people perceive you are competent, loving and caring, then they excuse one of life's little boo-boos now and then. You have to build the credibility and show everyone (your spouse, or the coach) that you have their best interests at heart. Show them that you are trying your hardest, that you really, really care.

I told Gene Keady (Purdue Head Coach) one night after he questioned a call I made that I might have missed it, but "I did not miss it in my heart." Those words just came out of my mouth, I am not sure why. But he liked it. He knew what I meant. He snarled, per usual, but he gave me some rope, gave me a chance, and he let it go.

In 2008, I worked the Tennessee-Kansas game, on ESPN national television, at Allen Fieldhouse in Lawrence, Kansas. It was packed, as always, one of the best venues in all of college hoops. Bruce Pearl coached Tennessee and Bill Self was at Kansas, just coming off a national championship year. It was a huge intersectional game. I officiated the game with a young official named

James Breeding, a really, really good up-and-coming official.

James was a good and conscientious guy. In the middle of the first half, James called an illegal screen that went against Kansas. Bill Self lost it. He went crazy over the call, just thought it was awful. And, he wouldn't stop. He gave James an earful. James walked away, the right thing to do, to let Bill vent. I assumed James knew the call was a 50/50 call and that he wasn't completely comfortable with it so he did not want to make a tough situation any worse. After a couple of trips up and down the court and the subsequent dead ball, I finally went over to Coach Self. He had to stop with his antics and complaining.

I had worked Bill's games at Tulsa, then at Illinois and at Kansas. We knew each other well and I knew he respected me. And, I respected him. We had been through a few tough moments together, one at Wisconsin when Bill was at Illinois that Bill is still mad about to this day; but he is a true gentleman and a great coach. I knew this had to stop and it was up to me to stop it. I said in a firm and friendly way, "Coach, you have to stop. The call was a tough one. There is a lot of game left. You have to let it go." That didn't do it. He kept complaining.

I finally looked him in the eye and said, "Bill, if you don't stop, this is only going to get worse. I am going to have to give you a technical foul. The way you are acting is hurting your team. You cannot act like this anymore. And, if you don't stop, I am going to give you a second technical and you will have to go out of here, in front of your home fans, thrown out on national TV. Stop, please." And, he stopped. He went back to coaching his team. He trusted me. He knew I had drawn a line in the sand. His perception of me was that I was doing what I had to do.

When I got home on Tuesday, after a couple of other games on the road, there was a handwritten note from Coach Self. He wrote: "Rick, I am sorry. I acted stupid on Saturday. James' call was correct. And, thanks for not throwing me out. Have a great rest of the year." Throwing him out was the last resort. But I would have done it and Coach Self knew that.

Late in the 1990s, I officiated a number of the University of Cincinnati games, with the volatile Bob Huggins as the head coach. I liked Bob, considering him a "man's man."

He says what he has to say, gets it out of his system, uses some tough language, but is very fair. He always respected me, for a variety of reasons.

Eldon Miller, a longtime coach at Ohio State, then at Northern Iowa, was a close friend of Huggins and had hired him as his assistant at the start of Huggins career. I worked a lot of his games over the years, some in tough circumstances — at Louisville, Memphis and at North Carolina.

That mutual relationship with Coach Miller gave me a chance to build a working relationship with Bob. He trusted me. I talked to him man to man. On this night, he got really upset with one of my partners and he just would not stop cursing and yelling at my partner. I went to that partner and said, "Look, you have to do something to stop Huggins. He won't stop until you address him, face to face." You have to call your own technical fouls. That is the only way to gain credibility with coaches.

I said to my partner, "If you don't take care of it, I will have to." And he said back to me, "Why don't you go ahead?"

That meant he did not want to do it. I understood, no problem. Not all of us are cut from the same cloth.

My partner didn't like to call technicals. Some guys just don't, for whatever reason. I did what I had to do, and gave a technical foul to Coach Huggins.

After I called it and we shot the two free throws, Bob yelled at me, "I am damn glad you are here, at least you have the courage to put me in my place. Thanks." And, he calmed down and it was over. His perception of me was that I would do what I had to do to make the game work, to make it fair. He was right. The way he was acting was not good for the game, it was not fair to the other coach or team and it was not right for my partner. I did what I had to do.

Positive perceptions are created in many ways. You can use tone of voice to your advantage. How you carry yourself builds your image with others. There are multiple ways to indicate you are listening intently to others. Each of these techniques builds your standing, increases the positive perception others have of you.

In basketball officiating, I have found working with a coach by giving him options is a great way to build a stronger relationship.

I have done this many, many times. Late in the game, when the ball goes out of bounds under the basket and stays with the offensive team, I will go directly to the head coach and say, "Which side do you want to take the ball out on?" The side doesn't matter to me, the ball went out in the middle. Either side is acceptable.

Every time, the coach looks and nods, because he knows you don't have to do that, you could just pick a side, tell them where it was going and they had no choice but to comply. In this case, credibility is built by giving them the choice. That builds credibility because you show that you care about them.

It's the little things like this that often build positive perceptions of you. For me, it might be giving a coach a few extra seconds to get a sub in the game or have a player replace a contact lens. At work, it might be showing respect for your co-worker's time. The next time around, that coach or coworker knows you run a flexible ship, responsive to others. They perceive you as fair. That builds your credibility. ■

Chapter 9 Lessons

1. The way the message is delivered is more important than the content — the package is more important than what is inside.

2. You are perceived by where you've been, how you look, the friends you keep. Bear that in mind, but don't let it completely define you. Work even harder the night after a big game or after you win a big assignment. Your fellow official or work colleague will be that much more appreciative of your effort.

3. Perception only takes you so far. Your actions also define the perception others have of you. If you fail to act, the perception others have of you weakens.

Chapter 10
Admit Mistakes

How many times in life have we looked back at a situation that occurred and said, "If I told the truth or admitted I was wrong at the beginning, this all could have been a lot easier on me."

I know I have. The cover-up is often a lot worse than the act itself.

Most people don't freely admit their mistakes.

We would do ourselves a huge favor if we would just go to our spouse or friend and just say, "I am sorry. I was wrong. I made a mistake or a bad judgment, I messed up. My fault, my mistake, I am responsible and want to apologize. I will do my very best to see that I do not repeat this behavior. If you will give me another chance, I will do my best to do better." People will almost always forgive you, and thank you for saying you were wrong. Their positive opinion of you grows.

We live in a forgiving society, one that wants to give second chances. I have raised three kids — my rule with them was the same: "Tell me the truth about what happened and we will figure out a way to make it better. But, don't lie to or try to hide the truth. That will cause serious issues and result in major consequences." To this day, I don't think any of the three have ever lied to cover up the truth.

The same principles apply in basketball officiating. You gain ground, respect and future goodwill if you say you were wrong and admit your mistakes. And, it will happen.

Admitting a mistake lets people know you are human. In basketball officiating, admitting a mistake lets others know you are not just a non-caring machine, out to make a paycheck, but that you hold yourself accountable, at a high standard, for what type of work you do on a nightly basis.

Fans, coaches, players, administrators and your supervisors want to know that you care. There are a lot of ways to show that you care about the game: Telling the truth to your supervisor when you get in a bad situation, being honest with your partner about what you saw, and not just giving the company line or what they want to hear, or admitting you made a mistake, you blew the play, you were wrong. Tell a coach you missed a play.

I have some standard responses if a coach wants to talk about a play he believes an official missed. "Coach, it's November. I am going to miss a play or two." "I missed the play, my fault." I am responsible, don't blame my partner." "We saw it differently, you may be right. Do you really think so?" "Tough play to call, maybe you are right."

These lines almost always illicit a positive response. There is seldom blowback afterwards.

Those types of admissions build credibility and connections, whether it's with a coach or how you approach a coworker, boss or employee in the workplace. Admitting the mistake and accepting responsibility disarms others. Still, the admission has to come from the responsible person for it to mean anything. If a coach goes after one of my partners, I do everything I can to have his back.

I will stand up for him, but do that by not trying to talk too much. Each official has to be the one to own up to their situation or mistake. It doesn't work any other way. If a coach questions me about a partner's call, I'll say, "Coach he will be over here in just a minute and you can talk to him then." And, then I move on. I never try to answer for someone else or try to explain their calls. It looks bad. It feels bad. And, to sell your partner out is unacceptable.

There is nothing worse during a game than to see your partner talking to one of the coaches and assuming they are talking about you, or one of your calls. That is an unwritten rule in officiating: Never sell your partner out. When someone gets the reputation among other officials that he does that, and there are some guys who do, they are not very popular. No one wants to work with them. I have broken up more than one fight in the locker room after games when just that issue was the cause. That is a no-no.

One night at Maryland, when Bill Guthridge had just taken over for Dean Smith at North Carolina, I had a free throw lane violation against Maryland that was minor, didn't impact the play, but should have been called. I knew it right away and immediately went to Coach Guthridge.

I had the ultimate respect for him, and said, "Bill, we had a free throw violation on that last free throw that I should have called, and I didn't. I am sorry." He looked right at me and said, "Rick, I should have gotten us out of this zone defense about four trips ago, don't worry about it." He winked at me. I will never forget it. What a first class response to my admission of an error, from a first class guy.

Indiana (and then Texas Tech) Coach Bobby Knight was a guy that I got along great with for some reason. He bought my act. I understood him. You could tell him you were wrong and he would take it from you and just sit down. You were accountable, you showed you cared. You talked to him man-to-man, and that was good enough for him.

One night at Northwestern, Indiana (IU) and Knight were playing a Big Ten game against the Wildcats. Tom Coverdale, an IU guard went to the basket, and extended his lead arm and knocked the Northwestern defender backward.

I was a tick late, but called an offensive foul on Coverdale. Knight screamed at me that the call was late. I yelled back, "It was late, but it was right." Knight cracked a smile and said, "Would you have told me if you thought you had missed the play?"

"Yup, but I didn't miss this one," I replied.

As always, to get the last word, Knight said, "You are one of the few who tell me when you screw up, but you do it so often I'm tired of hearing it."

If you admit too many mistakes, there's a problem. You won't be officiating much longer. You won't be leading the sales team in the future. Or your relationship isn't going to work out. If you find you are repeatedly admitting mistakes, you better take a long hard look at yourself and figure out what is wrong, because something is. Admitting the occasional mistake lets the official concentrate on his role. Admitting your mistakes in life or on the court shows you are accountable, that you care, that you are human, and things really do matter to you.

If you admit a mistake before the storm hits, you can prevent the worst effects from over-taking the game. If you wait too long, then troubles magnify. I messed up a play at Virginia one night, and on the way to the car I already had the cell phone dialed to my supervisor. I was going to get way ahead of the storm, and tell him exactly what happened before he heard it from someone else. I knew I messed up, and in some trouble, but the story was going to come from me.

At Virginia in mid-1990s, I was assigned the Duke-Virginia game with Tim Higgins and Zelton Steed.

Tim was a fabulous official and 'Z' is excellent as well. This was a great game at the old University Hall, packed. National television. Duke, with Coach K and his usual group of great players, brought out the best in every opponent, it seemed. This particular Virginia team was coached by Jeff Jones and the Director of Athletics at the time was the former great coach there, Terry Holland. Class guys, great school, wonderful atmosphere, big game.

We had a super game. No issues, we had it nailed all night long. But, you have to stay engaged for 40 minutes, not 39:53.

On this night, the most unfortunate set of circumstances unfolded. Virginia was up by one, with seven seconds to go. Higgins called a foul on Duke to put Virginia on the line, for two shots, up by one point. I was in the trail position by the scorer's table. Z was in the lead position administering the free throw. As the free thrower got ready to shoot the first free throw, Coach Jones sent a sub to the table to report into the game. But he decided he did not want him in until after the first free throw. I acknowledged the fact that he was there and notified Zelton of that fact, so the sub went back to the bench.

We shot the first free throw which was a terrible clunker of a miss, not even close. I heard Coach K instruct Steve Wojciech-owski (Wojo), his All-American point guard, "We have no time outs left. On the miss, you get the ball and push it down court as fast as you can and take it to the basket, make a play." So, I was prepared. Before the second shot, Coach Jones sent the same sub back to the table to come in after the second free throw, if it was made. I saw the sub.

The second free throw clunked around the rim and bounced up and around. I checked the table quickly, and found no sub waiting. The ball miraculously went in the basket. That created a dead ball situation, allowing a sub to enter. However, the horn did not blow to let the sub in. I didn't blow the whistle to let the sub in. I hustled down court to get ahead of what I knew was coming from the talk I overheard between Coach K and Wojo. Wojo was coming at me, and all hell broke loose. The table tossed a towel on the court to get the officials attention, but it was too late.

The sub should have come in after the made second shot. He did not. Wojo came to the basket.

To really finish off a horrible situation, I call a weak (and I mean soft and weak) foul on Virginia to put Wojo on the line to shoot two. Duke was down two points. Wojo was not a particularly great free throw shooter. I was praying for a miss. If he misses one then the game is over, Virginia wins, we escape even though we (I) messed up by not getting the sub in the game. Murphy's Law takes over, as it does inevitably for referees. Wojo makes two. Overtime. Duke wins in overtime.

We got to the locker room after the game and I was despondent. I screwed up as an individual and we had screwed up as a crew. I knew we were in trouble. Our supervisor, Fred Barakat, was a great man and a tremendous supervisor. But he expected excellence, especially from the three of us. He would never have expected a mess-up with the three of us in the game. Higgins looked at me and said, "Well, I think we are all right on that deal." I immediately looked at him and Zelton and said, "Oh, no, we are not okay. I am in deep sh*t. And, you guys are going to be with me. This is not going to be good at all." I knew it. We messed it up. But I was ultimately responsible, and had to get ahead of it. I called Fred immediately when we got in the car. He was steaming. I took a verbal beating, but admitted my mistake, and told the story just as I have told it here, taking my punishment, verbal and otherwise.

*　*　*

A funny aside to this game story: my daughter, Amanda, rode with me to this game. She was about 10 or so at the time and loved ACC basketball. After the game and on the way out of the arena, I grabbed Amanda by the hand and said to her, "Hold my hand. Look straight ahead. Do not make eye contact with anyone. Do not say a word, period. These people want to hurt your daddy. I will explain when we get to the car." We talk about this incident to this day. It really had an impact on Amanda.

*　*　*

Because I told the truth, both Jeff Jones and Terry Holland, though upset, supported me. To this day, I have not forgotten that support. Because I told the truth, admitted the mistake, and because the Virginia people were supportive, Fred Barakat eventually supported me as well.

All three of us got suspended for a game in the ACC and they made a big announcement about that. But, they sent us to the Big East for a game during the suspension, so we did not lose a check. That was nice. A great lesson learned all the way around. And, in the past 20 years, no official has forgotten a sub at the table since.

When that inevitable mistake comes on the court, I go to the coach immediately. I may run right to him and let my partners switch around me. Or, I might go to him on a dead ball, and say, "Coach, I missed the play. My mistake. I thought I saw his pivot foot move, it didn't, I was wrong." And, then I move on, get away. Get ahead of the tough situations in life by admitting you made a mistake. The game, or your life will flow a lot easier.

In the officiating business, no matter what sport, you have to be absolutely certain that you work the game from start to finish. Every game official has worked a game where they were nearly perfect for the first 39:48 of a basketball game or the first 59:45 of a football game, only to have something terrible happen in the last seconds of the contest that ruined the "perfect" game. One lapse in concentration or a lack of paying attention to all the important things down the stretch of a game is vital to success. Sometimes you get mesmerized by how good things have gone, or how great a job your partners are doing, or just how well-played the game has been. Then, "ka-pow," something happens that you never expected, or that surprises you and the "perfect" game is all messed up. That is a nightmarish situation and most of the time, can be avoided. You have to concentrate. You cannot be distracted or surprised. You must rely on your preparation to get you through. But, never, ever, can you relax. It isn't over until it is over! ■

Chapter 10 Lessons

1. By admitting your mistake, you indicate that getting the situation or play correct is what matters most. Others respect you for that. The admission is far better than the cover-up, which just implies guilt, and makes the situation worse over a longer period of time.

2. If you are repeatedly admitting mistakes, something is wrong. Analyze the problem. Take steps to fix it. Or you might be in the wrong profession.

3. Admitting mistakes quickly allows all parties to move on. Cleaning up the mess before the storm hits prevents a massive retroactive response.

Chapter 11
Enforce or Enable

I have two adult children now, Nate and Amanda. They are both unique and beautiful in their own way, and I have a deep love for them. Nate was adopted from El Salvador when he was nine months old.

His mom (Kathy) and I went through a long and involved process to get his adoption done and we went to San Salvador to pick him up. We brought Nathaniel (Nate) back to Iowa to live and he has turned into an excellent adult. However, at the start of his life he was a real challenge to raise, like many young children. Amanda followed Nate by 10 months so we went from zero kids to two, in less than a year. Challenging times for two graduate school students at the University of Iowa.

During meal time, one of Nate's favorite things was to pick up a pea, or a piece of corn, and throw it at his sister. He was really good at it. He threw accurate fastballs. This did not sit well with me, Kathy or Amanda, even though the clan could find it amusing.

After a number of incidents, I knew it was time to enforce discipline or enable Nate's behavior to continue and get worse.

"Nate, stop, don't do that," I said, "Nate, stop throwing peas at your sister."

I kept saying it and Nate kept winging the peas. So, it was time for old dad to tell Nate that if he kept throwing peas at his sister that he would go to his room for the night, with no dinner. He threw another and looked right at me.

I can remember it like it was yesterday: The first big test. What are you going to do, dad? Are you going to just tell me not to do it again? Are you going to ignore this behavior? Or, are you going to take action. I took action. I got Nate out of his chair and he went to his room, with no supper (what we call it in Iowa). He was not happy. But, throwing peas at the dinner table stopped forever. Enforce or enable. Pretty simple, right?.

Enforcement matters in life and officiating on the basketball court. It matters a lot.

If you want to clean up heavy contact between two post players, you must draw the line in the sand. Almost every night, post players see just how far an official will let them go.

I believe they should be able to play, and use their physicality, but it must be within the rules and fair for both guys. There is no penalty for being bigger or stronger or jumping higher than your opponent. However, play outside the rules, and you have to be penalized. My usual mode of operation with the post players is this: Use some "preventive officiating" to talk to them in hopes of keeping them out of a foul or two.

"Keep your hands off each other," "play legal," "stay straight up," "get out of the lane," "easy, now," are all phrases that I use to post players to see if I can help them play in a way that does not result in cheap fouls being called. I often bring the two post players together at a free throw or dead ball for a verbal message, "Listen, I do not want to call cheap fouls on either of you. I want you to play and not sit on the bench. This game needs you in it. Your team needs you. Your coach needs you. The fans want to watch you. So, if you will listen to me and play legal, we all will be better off, right? And, your coach won't be mad at you or me."

I draw a line in the sand, with a little humor. If the players keep it up, I blow the whistle.

Typically, I find after the first little talk when one of the post guys pushes, or holds, or chucks, or backs an opponent down, then a foul has to be called. There can be no more leeway given. I set the parameters, and enforced them.

As a guy who worked a lot of TV games, I felt an enormous responsibility to my particular supervisor to get the game right. They have a staff of young guys watching who get really confused if the game is worked differently every night. What do they call when they get the chance? You have to enforce the rules as written, with just a little bit of advantage/disadvantage and common sense sprinkled in to the equation.

When it comes to enforcement, you can't move the line in the sand. You cannot erase it and move it back.

I applied the same enforcement lessons to coaches, "Look coach, I have heard what you have said. I get it. Now, let it go. No more. Enough, that's it."

I draw the line in the sand. If the behavior continues, it's a technical foul. Enforcement builds respect. If you don't enforce, then weakness is detected and it is like blood in the water to a shark. Coaches want any advantage they can get. I like coaches, a lot. I enjoy talking to them and joking. But I know when game time comes, it is simple — they want a call. They want the game to go their way. All the good guy stuff goes out the window then.

I believe everyone likes to know their limits. How far can we go in a situation before crossing the line? I also believe that every young person wants discipline. They want to know the limits, they want parents to enforce and give some structure to their lives. They will respond positively to discipline.

Too many parents, coaches (referees) want to be friends. It does not work that way. It is hard to enforce, because it likely means telling friends or loved ones some things they do not want to hear or they disagree with. It can take a toll on your relationship. If you are the enforcer, you are the bad guy. It is not the policeman's fault he stopped you for speeding — you were driving too fast. It is not my fault we are having an intervention, you're using drugs. It is not the referee's fault he called a foul, you broke the rules, you ignored my words of warning. The policeman, partner or referee is not the bad guy.

I understand that people respond to strength, and kids want discipline and boundaries — it is in their DNA. I know this applies to coaches as well.

If you continue to say "that's enough, no more" and you do not take action, then it will never stop. You must take action. You either enforce or you end up enabling bad behavior. Nearly all NCAA Division I college basketball coaches have really strong personalities. They know you have a job to do. And you know that they have a job to do. But if you let them go, they will run over you to try and get another win. You have to stop that.

Tubby Smith is one of my favorite coaches, an "all-time good guy, and great with referees." I actually hired Tubby once at the University of Maryland-Baltimore, to be our head basketball coach, but circumstances intervened and we couldn't bring him on. I always tell Tubby that I was the first one to recognize his genius.

When Tubby took the Texas Tech head coaching job, it was his first time in the deep south after his stints at Kentucky and Minnesota.

All the referees knew him and loved him. Good guy, fair, honest, a man's man.

On this occasion, one of my partner's did the almost impossible and got under Tubby's skin somehow. I didn't know what had happened. We had all seen that Tubby Smith 'stare' which was usually directed at his players; only on a rare occasion was it directed at one of the referees. This was that rare occasion. Tubby was mad at my partner. He stared, stomped and yelled. He took a verbal shot at the guy when he ran by. You usually know when your partner knows he has messed up because he won't take action. He will give a lot of rope, letting a coach vent. That usually means your partner said something he should not have said. His lack of action is him trying not to make a bad situation even worse.

Tubby would not stop. I finally went over to Tubby and said, "Talk to me." That is the universal statement for trying to get a coach to tell you what is wrong and that you want to help make this better.

Tubby said, "Look, you didn't do anything, I am mad at your partner. He told me to sit down and be quiet. And, he was rude to my assistants. He didn't treat them professionally, and I don't appreciate it. It isn't right."

I agreed. Tubby was right. But, I told him he had to let it go and get back to coaching his team. Move on.

"Nope, I won't," was Tubby's response. I knew immediately this was not going to end well, and asked him once more to stop and then the ball was in play so I got into my position.

Tubby was right, he wouldn't stop. I went over again, and said, "Tubby, that is enough. No more. Go back to coaching. Let it go. If you don't then I am going to take care of this situation myself. Got it?"

No response. I had drawn the line. As I walked away, Tubby said, "I will let it go but your partner is horsebleep." I stopped, turned, and called a technical foul. It had to be done. I didn't like it, but I'd drawn the line. Enforce or enable.

In Tubby's defense, he was right. My partner, at least on that night, was horsebleep. But, he knew he couldn't say that and he knew I had a partner to protect.

On occasion, people can get carried away with enforcement. When I was the Director of Athletics at University of Northern Iowa (UNI), the university hosted several big name concerts in the UNI-Dome.

We provided some great entertainment for our community, state and students, and we made some good money by having Kenny Chesney, Nellie, the Black Eyed Peas, Trace Adkins and many other groups in concert. We had a lot of fun doing this. One afternoon, prior to one of these concerts, I was in my office and the phone rang. It was one of my assistant athletic directors who asked me if I could come down to our strength and conditioning facility, there was a problem.

"You are going to laugh," she said, "but we need you down here."

I went down to the facility. At the door stood my strength and conditioning coach, his assistant AD, and Kenny Chesney, the great country singer.

We had Chesney for concerts three times and he sold them out. He was a money maker for us, and our facility for him. He was a good guy and liked to work out and play basketball on concert days, and we happily obliged him. This was about 4 p.m. in the afternoon and our weight room was full of our volleyball and football players, getting in their lifting work. Chesney had come to the weight room to workout, and our strength and conditioning guy, enforcing the rules that no one gets in except those scheduled to work out, would not let Chesney in.

Our strength and conditioning guy told Chesney no one gets in except the teams that are scheduled, no exceptions. Chesney explained that he was with the concert at the Dome that night. Still the answer was no. Finally, exasperated, Chesney said, "I am the concert, I am Kenny Chesney." Even that didn't matter; my strength coach would not let him in, saying, "I don't care who you are, our rules are our rules." That is when I arrived, heard the story and even though it was hard to keep a straight face, I took the strength coach aside. I explained that it would be a really cool thing for the kids to get to lift with Kenny, it would be a lifetime memory. Maybe we could put a little of his music on the speaker system, have a little fun. Take some pictures, use them for recruiting. Maybe ease the enforcement rules a bit. He really didn't have a choice, that is what we were going to do, but I wanted his buy-in. With a little arm-twisting, he agreed. No one else was allowed in the room and the party started.

Sometimes a basketball official must pull out some little tricks to make the game work. Every few games you'll have one where both teams seem out of sorts on the court. Players complain about every play. Sometimes that is just the culture of the team. Or it is what they see from their coach. In those situations, I will often say something like this at a free throw, (when you have seven or eight guys within an area where they can hear you) "Listen, the next guy on either team who complains about a call in any fashion will get a technical foul. Does everyone understand?"

The line is drawn. Everyone heard you. The next time someone even wrinkles up their nose in regard to any call — technical foul. It works every time.

I will use the same situation at the free throw line for another lesson on enforcement, "Listen number 21, you have refereed your last play. You play, and we will referee. But you are not going to do both things. Got it? Next time it is a technical foul."

The line is drawn. Everyone hears it. The player either stops the bad behavior or he gets penalized. It is about 70/30 on what happens. Some guys get it and stop. Some guys never get it and react negatively. Then you penalize. If you don't, then you lose all credibility with those players. And, not just for that night, for a long, long time. They remember you and the fact that all you did was warn them, you never enforced.

One of my favorite and fun things to do now and then is when two players are getting after each other — trash talking or putting some junk in the game. I call one of them aside and say, "Listen, you are the best player on the court tonight. That is a big responsibility. You have to act like you are the best player on the court. Don't let number 23 bother you. He couldn't guard you with a tent. You are so much better than him it is crazy. Act like it, okay?"

Invariably, I find the player will tell me I am right and he will puff out his chest and give me a pat on the back. It's all good. Then I will go to the opposing player, the one he has been mixing it up with, and I will say the exact same thing. Tell him how great he is. How the other guy cannot possibly guard him and so on. Same thing happens. Chest out, "you are right ref," comment, and a smile. Situation mitigated. No need to worry about those two anymore. On to the next battle. Enforce or enable.

Enforcement establishes discipline. It sets the boundaries, let's everyone know you are serious, that you have a limit to what you will tolerate. It garners respect and builds relationships by showing strength. It means that you are going to get the job done and that you are not someone who can be messed with.

In life, it means you love someone but you will not let their behavior ruin them, or negatively impact you or your family. You will draw a line as to what is acceptable behavior and then you will take action when that line is crossed. There will be consequences to behavior that is inappropriate. That shows strength. That shows love. And it shows that you will not enable them and their inappropriate behavior. You will enforce. ■

Chapter 11 Lessons

1. Enforcement is successful because of follow through. Set the parameters. Establish the punishment, fine or penalty. Then follow through. Positive results follow.

2. Enforcement builds respect. In parenting, business or officiating, when others see you as someone who enforces the rules fairly and without prejudice, you gain respect. When you don't enforce, people use that as leverage against you.

3. Draw a line in the sand. Don't move it. Enforce it. (Unless it is Kenny Chesney in question and then maybe a little wiggle room is appropriate.)

Chapter 12
Be an Artist, Not a Scientist

I consider Tim Higgins, a fellow referee, the best of our generation — a quality dad, husband and funny guy always ready with a quip. Higgins hails from New Jersey, and worked a full-time job in New York City while officiating, and continues to do so today after retiring from running the hardwood. He knew how to survive and do this refereeing job with a personal and gentle touch.

He almost never had to get out the "discipline stick" because he had universal trust and could communicate his way out of any sticky situation that his partner (usually) or Tim himself (rarely) had created. He was an artist on the basketball court. His body was not the greatest; his hair was not perfect, he did not run beautifully. He knew the rules, but more importantly he knew what was right to do. He managed the game and communicated better than anyone. I can still see him talking to a coach, with his hand covering his mouth so no one could hear them. Then I can see the laugh between them and the coach patting Tim on the back. Everything was okay. They trusted a true artist who did what he had to do to make the game work for everyone.

It is impossible to quantify life or a basketball game. Neither are perfect. Some things just are not exactly right, by the book, one way or another. There are shades of grey, some absolutes and things that never change, but not many. Solutions are often complicated. Life and basketball are not exact science. Artists paint pictures, sing or dance expressively. You cannot be a cookie cutter person. To be great, you have to be flexible, extemporaneous, true to yourself, creative and have a huge imagination. Walk with the elephants now and then. Go outside what is the norm.

Hank Nichols, the long time and outstanding Division I college basketball referee and later the national coordinator for college basketball, always talked about officiating as an art. There was not one particular way to do it. You had to be yourself, yet follow and enforce the rules, handle the absolute plays. He coached officials to understand what was an advantage and what was not an advantage on a particular play. He used to say that refereeing the game was like playing an accordion. In order to make beautiful music on the accordion you had to let it way out and bring it way in and go back and forth and let the accordion do its job.

So it is in basketball games. Sometimes you have to call the game very close and quickly do that because of the style of play, the rivalry or the temperature of the coaches. At other times, you can let the game flow on its own, with many fewer whistles and stoppages. You can be prepared and watch film and do everything possible to be ready but each situation that comes up is unique and has to be dealt with that way.

It never fails, and it always makes me laugh. The television announcers will say 'Well, they are really letting them play tonight," or "Wow, they are calling it close tonight." Every game is different. Every game needs an artist's touch, not a scientist's exactness.

I worked for many years in the old Big East. Any official from that league will tell you how tough and physical those games could be.

Every night, every game seemed impossible. Rivalries ran rampant, big name coaches stalked the sidelines. Great players ran the court in old and storied venues.

And some great — and I mean great — officials worked that league. Some of them were not household names (Joe Mingle, Jackie Hannon, Pete Pavia) but they were guys who could really officiate. Sometimes you just worked by the seat of your pants, did what you had to do. Mechanics and how you looked or ran or your reputation outside of the Big East were irrelevant. But I learned more about surviving there than I did anywhere else.

I saw one of the top-rated ACC officials come to the Big East one year, his first in the league. He had a 25 game schedule in the Big East and he deserved it — he had the credentials. He worked four games of that schedule and said, "The hell with this" and turned all his Big East games back in. That league was not for everybody. I remember before games in the Big East going into the officials' locker room and looking in the mirror and telling myself that the good old Midwestern boy, gentle and kind and loving, wasn't going to work tonight. Put on your hard-core, no B.S. game face and go to work. It was the only way you could survive.

One night in the early 1990s, I worked my first league game in the Big East — in Madison Square Garden in New York City. An Iowa farm boy was getting a shot in the world's most famous arena. It was a big deal for me just to find the Garden, get in the elevator and to the locker room. The game was St. John's vs. Hall, a rivalry that included Coach P.J. Carlissimo of Seton Hall, who didn't say much, but who respected officials, and was in turn respected by them.

On one play in the early stages of the game, the St. John's dribbler brought the ball to mid-court. As he got into front court, the Seton Hall defender hit him with a forearm to the hip so hard that he stepped into backcourt. I looked at the play and called a hand-checking foul, an easy call, so I thought. After reporting the foul, I looked up and P.J. was standing right directly in front of him: "Rick, what the hell was that?"

I was stunned. The call was easy and had to be made. No one could complain about it. I thought that if this call was in question, then I didn't belong in Big East basketball.

I replied to P.J., "Coach, he hit him so hard he stepped into backcourt. I had to call a foul. It is either a hand-check or a backcourt violation, I had to take one or the other."

P.J. looked at me and in 100 percent seriousness said, "Rick, this is the damn Big East. You ignore both of them and play on." P.J. expected artistry, not science. He expected you would apply your best judgment on every play and decide if there was an advantage or a disadvantage gained, then you would make your decision.

Officials do not have the advantage of slow motion on the court. Things happen extremely quickly in a small space with big, long, wide, powerful and fast athletes. You must rule instantaneously in real time and do it at a correct rate of 95 percent or so in order to continue to be employed. No matter how much video you watch or how much tape you break down or how many tapes you review, you cannot turn that into a science. It is an art form. You can look at a play a hundred times on video and the play will look different from different angles.

I had a play last year at Florida with a drive to the basket and Florida on defense. I was in the lead position, under the basket and in perfect position. I saw the entire play, called a blocking foul, the basket "good" and one free throw.

The place went up for grabs. I looked at a partner whom I trust implicitly, Tim Gattis, a great and underrated official. I could tell by his body language he thought I was wrong. The crowd thought I was wrong. Billy Donovan, the Florida coach, left no doubt that he thought I was wrong.

Florida went on to win the game. In the locker room after the game, the crew got the game video almost immediately on their iPad's (standard procedure). Don Rutledge, a long time great official and now an observer in the SEC, was there. They looked at the play together.

It was hard. It was very close. But at the very last second, the Florida defender slid to his right ever so slightly and moved to take the supposed charge. I was right. Not by much, but I was right. Why? It did not feel like a charge to me at the time of the play. No one is good enough to see that slight late movement. I could not apply science. It happened too fast. I could not go to the review; it is a judgment call and non-reviewable play.

I applied my years of experience and the artist in me, not the scientist, to call a play that I thought felt a certain way. You cannot teach that. There is no cut and dried way to know you will make a business decision correctly or an instantaneous ruling on the basketball court with the highest degree of accuracy.

Anyone who says that ability on the basketball court isn't an art form has never been on the big stage, operating at a speed beyond the comprehension of those who have not officiated at that level.

This is the great dilemma of officiating. We want you to call this play this way, every time, you are told. These plays are absolutes, they tell us. But what the higher ups forget is that they would NEVER have done that. If the game is 61-61 when Kansas plays at Kansas State and you call a tiny little hand check at the top of the key and end a classic game at the free throw line, you will be awfully lucky if your supervisor supports you and puts you back in a game like that. It is an art. No one wants a game to end like that.

A foul in the first 10 seconds is not always a foul in the last 10 seconds. Let's be practical. In a perfect world, yes, but you cannot referee these games in a vacuum. Let the players on the floor, within the scope of reasonable judgment, decide games. A touch foul, soft foul, bad whistle — none of those calls should ever determine a winner.

In life, business or on the basketball court, you can plan and prepare and have all sorts of goals, objectives and ways of measuring. In the end, it is the person who adapts to a changing environment, a changing set of circumstances who succeeds at the highest levels.

Prepare for different life situations. Working your way through these situations is an art form. You cannot use science to solve a relationship problem or to resolve an argument with a friend. You must apply your artistry to each particular situation. You have to get a feel for the situation and then use your experience and background and everything inside of you to do what is right, to make the situation right.

I am a huge Garth Brooks music fan. I love Brooks' lyrics. *Standing Outside the Fire* is one of his favorites, and I use words from it in speeches. I have been to a few of his concerts.

He's a great performer and an amazing artist because he steps outside what is expected or normal to do his thing. If he played music like a science—by the book—and with no margin for artistry, he would be boring and predictable. He is exciting, different, unique, talented and off-the-charts successful.

Life is not boring or predictable. Neither is basketball. Nor the artistry of officiating the game. ■

Chapter 12 Lessons

1. Sometimes you have to let some rope out, and other times tighten it up. There are no fast rules to predict every situation in life. Develop a feel to trust the artist inside you.

2. You cannot be taught to be an artist, but it can be refined. We all have a form of artistry inside. Cultivate it, and it will serve you well over the years.

3. Prepare for many different life situations and adapt as you go. That's the artist side of you growing from new circumstances.

Chapter 13
Objectively Evaluate Yourself

One of the hardest skills for anyone to master is self-evaluation. It is easy to see our strengths, but tougher to identify and pinpoint our weaknesses. It is even harder for most people to address those weaknesses through evaluation, a plan to address those weaknesses and then take action to change or grow.

"A day without some growth is a wasted day." It's a famous phrase from a Jim Valvano speech at the ESPY's right before his death from cancer — a remarkable statement from a remarkable man.

"Think, laugh and be moved to tears. That's a full day," Valvano told the audience that evening years ago.

All of us need things to dream about to get and keep us motivated. Dreams keep us alive. But unless we work on the things that are not our strengths, we cannot get better.

We need to ask ourselves every day, are we growing, getting better, moving forward, improving our relationships or our fitness or our lot in life, or not. If we are not moving forward and getting better, then we are getting worse, moving backwards. There is no status quo. There is no staying static. We all need goals and dreams and things to look forward to and then we need a plan to implement and make us better in all the areas of our life. An old coach I had used to say, "Either be a leader or get out of the way." He meant you had to get better or you hold things up.

Have you ever gone to a golf driving range to work on your game or watch a friend hit balls? Next time, take a look around. You will see any number of golfers who hit their driver to see how far they can smash the ball. Certainly, driving the ball off the tee is a key part of golf. It takes about 14 swings (or strokes) a round. Chipping and putting use up 40+ strokes a round.

Hmmm, what should we work on the most? Most people work on their strengths too much and their weaknesses not enough. Get academic help when you have trouble with a class or go to a therapist if you have issues in your life where you need to talk to someone. Admitting you have a problem is the first step to getting right again. The same goes for self-evaluation. If you identify your weak areas and then address them and try to make them better, then you make personal progress.

That can make you a better person, spouse, dad/mom, friend, worker or referee. But, it is very hard to do. Getting past the psychological hurdle that allows you to recognize that you have weaknesses to address is a start.

Many people spend a lot of time worrying or talking about other people and their perceived weaknesses. We need to concentrate on ourselves, our actions, our own personal strengths and weaknesses, no matter what area of our life we are considering.

I read a great quote once that I think of often: "Below average people talk about other people. Average people talk about things. Brilliant people talk about ideas." (Admiral Hyman Rickover)

That quote applies to self-evaluation. I know a number of people who fill their days worrying about everyone but themselves.

They talk and gossip about everyone else and they ignore how they could make the world (or their household) better. A trip to the mirror would help

If you find, through self-evaluation that you are not doing things that you need to do, what could happen? You could lose a valued relationship. You could lose your job. You could lose your basketball schedule. Or worse, you could lose your life or your ability to function in a way that allows you to have a high quality of life.

I talk to youth groups often. One of the things I stress to them is that they need to do their best to maintain a high level of physical fitness. They need to stay on top of what they eat, their exercise regimen, so they are doing these things right almost every day.

I find it sad seeing some people work their entire lives to have the money to do things, but they badly ignored their physical fitness. When they get to retirement, they cannot get around or they have so many aches and pains that getting out of the house is difficult.

We are living longer than ever, so it is incumbent upon each of us to self-evaluate our fitness, weight, eating habits and exercise plan to maximize our quality of life both for ourselves and for those who count on us.

I keep a personal list of things that are important to me, a diary of sorts, but not the kind where you write down page after page each day. I write notes to myself every day on things I need to pay careful attention to — a personal "to-do" list that not only involves "to-dos," but also things to think about and address. I have done this in my basketball officiating for years, keeping a list of all the plays that I felt I messed up or ones to think about before a new season or game so I don't make the same mistakes.

At this stage of my officiating career, it's a long, long list. For example, when a player jumps to shoot and then starts a dribble from the air, what is the call? Travel. Or what is the call when an offensive player goes up to shoot and the defender either caps (places his hand or hands on top of the ball) the ball and forces the offensive player back to the floor or just briefly touches the ball and the offensive player comes down with the ball? It's a very hard play to officiate and react to immediately with a high success ratio. I've messed it up more than once, and have dozens of these types of plays chronicled to review so I hopefully get them right the next time.

I have a list of reminders to consider before each game. For example, I always check the clocks before crossing the end line and half court line. If a team is going to take a foul, I make sure they foul before blowing the whistle. My notes tell me, "Do not anticipate a foul." I have tips to myself not to get surprised by play at the rim, to watch for offensive and defensive interference when the ball reaches that height. I have hundreds of those written down. The process of capturing past events, and learning from mistakes, increases the learning curve. This type of self-evaluation is critical for improvement.

Don't overdo your personal evaluation. It can paralyze you. Be realistic, establish personal standards and see how you don't measure up to those standards, then work on them. But find a way to move yourself forward and address your personal issues. You can be critical of yourself, that is okay, but do not be too tough on yourself. Give yourself some love.

You might need to lose 20 pounds. If you try to lose 10 pounds in a week, you will fail. You have to lose weight the same way you put it on, slowly, a little at a time. Make a smart plan for a nutrition change, drink a lot of water, burn off more calories than you take in, and you are on your way. But, your goals have to be realistic and you have to stay with it. There are no quick fixes.

Self-evaluation helps you improve on the status quo. With introspection and evaluation, we all can improve. It has to be realistic, and you have to stay with it. ■

Chapter 13 Lessons

1. Maintain a high level of physical fitness. It helps you perform at your peak, and bodes well for your later years. Re-evaluate that regime repeatedly.

2. In some way, shape or form, jot down notes for self-improvement. Capture situations where you learned something, or how you could improve. Read back over them periodically and commit to your mind to execute on these improvements the next time you are faced with a similar situation.

3. What would you do differently next time after you self-evaluate your performance? Challenge yourself, stretch your boundaries: Place yourself in a totally new environment and ask yourself, "How can I perform better?"

Chapter 14
Moving On

One of the obvious things about our lives is that what happens today, short of death, is not the end. Tomorrow will come, the sun will rise and set regardless of how great or bad your last day was. We have to be ready to move forward, take the next step, the next challenge and get past the good or bad that we just experienced. Many times we fail to celebrate the great successes in our lives; and we are often focused on the failures or bad things that happen for way too long. We need to process the experiences — good or bad. But we cannot let the celebration of the great things that happen nor the despair of the negative things that happen paralyze us. We must gather ourselves and move forward.

"Life goes on" is a statement we hear often. I think that trivializes the process, because life events are precious in many ways. But eventually life does go on, and we need to be prepared for that moving on process.

Whether it is a big basketball game (remember, every game is big to someone), a successful business deal, the birth of a child or any of so many great things that happen to people each day, the next step is crucial. There is <u>always</u> a next step.

One night in February 1998, I worked the North Carolina-Duke game in Durham, N.C. It was a classic, and I felt my crew did a good job in an extremely tough contest. I flew home, worked at my "real" job as the Director of Athletics at Bucknell the next day, then jumped in the car and drove to St. Francis of Pennsylvania, to officiate their game vs. Mt. St. Mary's.

I always try to work harder the night after a huge game when you knew many people saw you the night before. Duke versus North Carolina is obviously one of the biggest games of the year. But, Mt. St. Mary's at St. Francis was a big game for those kids, coaches and fans too. As we were officiating the first half that night, I heard a fan yell, "Hey Hartzell, you are not at Duke tonight!" Even though that was a reasonably benign comment and not something that bothered me at all, it did serve as a good wakeup call. One fan must have thought that I was not giving my best effort, or that I had a hangover from the night before and that was enough for me. Head down, concentrate, get in the moment, focus and move on from last night. Good lesson.

I have raised two great children who are now adults. That took place in a busy but great time in my life. I savored those moments even though I was trying to build a career in two areas (administration and refereeing). My kids have always been, and will always be, the most important aspect of my life. I would do anything for them, short of enabling bad behavior, to help them in their lives. Now I am raising two young sons from my second marriage. I have learned so much from this magical process — more patience and quality time. Though they all have different personalities, there is still my old school idea of good behavior — a firm handshake, a positive attitude every day and no whining.

Things are different for me today because I am older, wiser, the times have changed, the outside influences more immediate. I need to adjust, move forward, grow patience, learn new lessons to get better as a referee, husband and father.

Jackson is so happy and upbeat. And, he loves sports even though we have not pushed him in that direction. He has been around that atmosphere all his life so I guess it is osmosis that puts the sports bug in you. However, I want him to be a boy, so he has other interests. He likes movies and his X-Box, and playing with his young friends. He does not want to just shoot baskets all the time or hit the baseball. He wants to do Tae Kwan Do, swim, go see movies.

I had to adjust because all I wanted to do as a kid was play ball. Maybe that is because there was not much else to do on our farm in Klemme, Iowa. My mom always told me that she never had to worry about where I was because she could hear that basketball bouncing in our barn, where I had the greatest indoor basketball court ever. It was better once the cows started eating the hay because then I had more room to play, but I had my ball, my hoop, my court and my dream. I was Oscar Robertson and Lou Hudson and Pete Maravich. And that was enough for me. Not yet for Jackson.

That adjustment is up to old dad. I had to move on to foster Jackson's development and growth.

The life of an official in any sport is made up of missed calls. There are great games and near-perfect games. Sometimes your mistakes are so minor that no one knows they even happened. But, you learn from your mistakes. And, if you are any good at all, you use those mistakes to make you better the next night out.

I worked several Purdue vs. Indiana games in the 1990s and early 2000s, a very difficult game no matter where it is played. Bob Knight was going up against Gene Keady, an in-state rivalry, and often during those years for Big Ten supremacy. It was a super-charged atmosphere, a night I always looked forward to and savored.

On this particular night I was working with Tom O'Neill (an excellent official who's been to several Final Four's, and a dear friend) and a guy at the end of his career named Ed *(Editor's note: Some names have been changed in the writing of the book, including this one)*. Ed was a very good official. But he had not been in this environment much. I knew we were in trouble early when Ed announced to us that he had warned Knight. Ouch. To warn any coach that early in the game is usually a recipe for a big problem.

And, it was. Knight got a technical foul mid-way through the first half, a part of the game. The crew did a little adult day care to settle things down. I told Knight that he was probably going to get a technical foul sometime in the game anyway, so now it was over, talking him down off the ledge. Time to move on.

A couple minutes later, Ed called a backcourt foul against Indiana, a non-controversial ruling. But it was their seventh foul so the bonus was in effect. Purdue shot the one and one. I was in the trail position by the Indiana bench. Ed and O'Neill were administering the free throws.

Something felt wrong to me. One of Purdue's post players was shooting, and the foul occurred (I thought) on the dribbler for Purdue who was bringing the ball up the court. Before I could sort things out, the Indiana bench went crazy. Coach Knight and Dan Dakich were up in arms that we had the wrong free throw shooter at the line. The first free throw had already been shot and made. I was trying to keep peace at the bench. Remember, Bobby Knight already had a technical, so throwing him out was something to avoid if at all possible.

I asked him and Dan to calm down. Relax. Let me figure this

out. I will never forget what Knight said to me then: "Don't screw us again, okay?" Like I had before? Like the technical was my fault? I said I wouldn't do that, but he needed to give me a minute to sort this out. I asked Tom and Ed to wait a minute and went to the table.

The Indiana table was always great. They promised me we had the wrong shooter. I figured out who the right shooter was and quickly went to Tom, who was the administering official under the basket, getting ready to give the free thrower the ball for the second shot. He could not understand what I was doing. Why was I holding up the game? I tried to talk to Tom but it was so loud I had to get right in his face. And, what I said to him was inappropriate. Maybe not so inappropriate under normal conditions, but inappropriate with the television cameras on us and easy to read my lips and the inappropriate words I said to Tom right then: "We have the wrong !@#$%^&*()(*&^%$#@! shooter." Those were my words. I said them.

Under the circumstances, noise, frustration and pressure, it was probably not the worst thing a basketball official ever said on the court. But I knew the words were not appropriate, particularly on national television with a lot of people who didn't know me watching. And, it wasn't my true character to do that.

I try to comport myself like a professional at all times. I try not to lose my composure or say anything inappropriate on or off the court. What I'd said in the Indiana-Purdue game deeply bothered me.

We got the new shooter, got the game back under control and moved on. And Knight stayed until the end. It was a crazy night. But, we got in the car and I felt awful. I knew what had happened. I called my supervisor in the Big Ten, Rich Falk, one of the classiest guys ever. A pro's pro. I told him what I said and that it was on television and not only could you read my lips but maybe the audience could hear me too. I apologized. I wanted him to know that I felt awful. He was great about it, as always. He told me to call in the morning. The whole thing blew over with no real fanfare. Rich was great, as was Commissioner Jim Delany. But I was really mad at myself. That was not something I did— talk like that. And, it bothered me for a long time.

Despite my verbal mistake, I had been able to prevent a bigger mess from occurring. What I said was wrong, and I knew that. I had to process the event and promise myself no matter how difficult things were or how frustrated or irritated that I was at the time that I would never speak that way again where others might see or hear me.

I embarrassed myself, fell short of my standards. So, I made a promise that it would never happen again and to be certain starting the next night to never curse on the court for any reason to anyone at anytime. I have stuck to that, learned the lesson and moved on.

There is always a next step. There is always a next day, a next game. Part of the fun in life is preparing for that next step while understanding that we all mess up along the way. We develop from the good and the bad. Our progress as a person or mate or business person or official is shown only if we grow and develop from the good or the bad that happen to us. Experience it, process it, savor or get over it, and move on. It is our only choice. ■

Chapter 14 Lessons

1. To move up, you have to move on.

2. Take time to process your mistakes. Analyze them fully, get feedback from others. Talk it through. Then take positive steps to manage the situation better the next time.

3. There is always a next step, another game, a new goal. Experience each step along the way, process it, savor it or get over it, and move on.

Chapter 15
Not Being Number One

"We're number one, we're number one." So goes the chant of every fan of every team all across the United States, and many other parts of the world. It has been that way for a long time. Unfortunately, not every team or individual can be number one. Someone has to be second best or third best, or not good enough at all. Only one team or person can be number one. The rest of us are not number one.

The statement you hear in NASCAR terms — yes, I am a racing fan — is that "second place is the first loser." I am not a fan of that statement, but I understand the concept — win or nothing. Winning is not just important, it is the only thing that is important. Unfortunately for all of us, someone is always better. No matter how good we are, very seldom are we the very best, even for a short time. Tom Brady, in my opinion, is the best quarterback in the NFL. But a lot of guys are gaining on him. His window is tight and there is always someone who others think is better.

The guy who works the referee spot in the last game of the year, the championship game of the Final Four, is considered the best college basketball official for the season, but only for 40 minutes.

I remember growing up and facing a baseball pitcher from the town next to me. The opponent was bigger, stronger and faster, and he could throw "peas" up to the plate, even at age 10. I thought I would never be that good. But, the big kid changed and faded, and the other kids caught up.

My little guy, Jackson, wants to be Russell Wilson, LeBron James and Justin Verlander. Sometimes he does not practice as much as I think he should just to be reasonably good, much less the level he now dreams about. I tell him that "Somewhere, someone your age is practicing right now, trying to be the best they can be." Now, I don't want him to practice all the time. I want him to be a boy. He might not ever be number one, but the journey, the effort to get to that point is crucial. And, that is all I expect. His best. My best. And, hopefully that best is good enough. It might not make us number one, but all anyone can ask for is that championship effort.

Jackson loves Russell Wilson. He thinks Wilson is the best quarterback around and he can give you a dozen reasons why. He does not understand that not everyone thinks that Wilson is the best. Jackson thinks it is obvious. But, I have told him, "even Russell Wilson knows, in his heart, that he is not the best quarterback in the NFL. But he is close and he wants another title and that is what drives him. Whether he ever gets to that title or not, he is going to do all he can to try to get there." Not everyone is number one, but you must keep driving.

I never worked the Final Four for any level of men's college basketball. It is in the cards that I will never work the Final Four. I had several chances to make it, since I worked the regional (third and fourth round) 18 times in his career. But, I was never picked to be in that final group of officials.

I saw guys get picked who were not as good as me, or from another part of the country where they worked a schedule that paled in comparison to mine. I saw guys who were not in shape, or didn't care as much as I thought they should have. I saw guys make it who you knew were political choices. I saw guys make it who messed up games or who didn't blow the whistle at all, or who rode in on someone else's coattails to make it to the Holy Grail, the Final Four — every referee's dream. I worked all the big games, all the rivalries, in all the big arenas. I dealt with all the tough coaches, the pressure and scrutiny. I worked conference championship games by the dozens.

I am not mad at the guys who made it; I am happy for them. I am not mad at the people who selected them nor the process. I just know that I deserved to go. You cannot work the schedule I worked for as long as I worked it and not think that.

I made the NCAA tournament 23 times, so I was frequently in the conversation to be chosen for the last three games (semi-finals and final). I was one of the 96 best college basketball, and the top 36 and top 12, but never the top nine or number one. Did that make me a lesser official or man?

Everyone deals with disappointment differently. Success is defined by various measures. I have had an incredible run of success in officiating, but I wanted the BIG game. What didn't I do? What could I have done differently? What more could I have done?

I heard it all in terms of why I wasn't selected: "It's a conflict with your Athletic Director position; we don't need officials from your primary conference; you blew a call early in your career and can't be trusted."

I assumed ultimately I was not considered good enough by those doing the ranking. It was hard. It hurt me. I hated the week after the Regional each March because I knew I was going to get that call from the NCAA: "You did a great job. You were really good in your games. Very impressive. Thank you. We are not moving you forward." Same story every year. It got so they did not even need to say anything. In fact, one year, not trying to be a smart ass, but I said when the call came, "Let me guess, great job. I was awesome. Can't thank me enough. But not advancing." At least we could laugh about that.

I knew I was good enough. My peers knew I was good enough. In fact, a lot of them still tell me and Mike Wood that we were the best two referees never to make the Final Four. Neither Mike nor I get much solace out of that. But, I got over it and moved on. I know in my heart that I was good enough. The fact that I was not number one — that was okay.

Oddly, being good enough doesn't always make a person, team or company number one. Being the best candidate doesn't elect someone as president or decide who gets to be CEO of Microsoft. There are many talented people for top positions in every field, but only one person ascends that ladder. The others are not losers. Companies in every line of business grow annually and have happy customers, but they may not have the most sales or steepest year-to-year increases. Only one team wins the college basketball championship each year. All the others had differing levels of success and joy along the way. Teams, businesses and individuals all have different success paths, but it doesn't mean "having to be number one."

It took me awhile to figure this out. I grew up in a town of 600 people with a graduating class of 36, on a farm where I did not go west of the Missouri River or east of the Mississippi River until I was 17. The farm had outdoor plumbing for a majority of my youth.

Over the years, I found my image of getting to the top or "being number one" changing, understanding that I was luckier in officiating than I was good. I got to do what thousands of guys would loved to have done. I saw hundreds and hundreds of guys come and go. Many of them were much more talented than me. But, they did not get the chance to do what I did — officiate the top games in big-time venues with great partners.

For the 1990s and early 2000's, I worked a full schedule and turned games down in the best leagues. I did a lot with what God gave me. And, no one remembers who worked the Final Four years later anyway. I was always disappointed when I didn't go. But, when I put it in perspective and looked around the room at my peers, family, house, real job, and my faith, I was good with the way things turned out.

Fulfillment comes with age. So does cynicism. Someone once told me that when you become cynical and negative then you are getting old. I refuse to go down that path.

It is going to take a lot more than not getting some basketball assignment to get me down and make me act stupid. Now, I don't even think about the games I get or where they are or how important someone else thinks they are. I know they are important to someone, so I make them important to me. And, I savor those games and those chances to work because they are coming to an end. I have had a tremendous run. It is just about time to turn the page and let someone else do it.

No one will take away my memories of Kentucky vs. Kansas in the Louisiana Superdome during the regional round of the NCAA Tournament. Or Texas El-Paso vs. Indiana (Knight vs. Haskins, my first NCAA Tournament game) or Syracuse (with Carmelo Anthony) vs. Auburn in Albany, N.Y., the year Syracuse won it all. Or Florida vs. Gonzaga in Phoenix, when I made a "must" call at the end.

Was I technically ever number one? No, probably not. But I

carved my own path, found my niche.

In 2007, my supervisor in the Horizon League, John Adams, took over the NCAA supervisor position, selecting officials for the NCAA tournament. I had worked eight consecutive Horizon League championship games for John.

He trusted me. I gave him a lot of nights where I could have officiated elsewhere for more money or prestige and I worked for him and the Horizon League instead. I could get home most nights and they paid decently. It was nice to get the championship game repeatedly. So, when John got the NCAA job, I thought my time had finally arrived.

When the NCAA tournament rolled around, I got two games the first weekend in Minneapolis, and did well. I was then assigned the Regional in Boston — Pittsburgh vs. Dayton, with fellow officials Bob Donato and Joe Lindsay. I was the referee.

It was a great assignment, excellent game, and we came through with flying colors. Bob and Joe were terrific, and I felt I had done extremely well, which meant there was a chance to move on. The Regional ended and I went home and tried to stay busy. I was outside working on a race car we had at the time the call came. I saw the call was from John Adams and it was a Monday night. I finally got the call. *This was it. My time. My family and I could go to the Final Four and I would work a game, I did not care at all which game, I was in. Wow.* I answered the phone. John said, matter-of-factly, "You are one of 19 guys recommended to work the Final Four. Congratulations." I was in heaven. *Finally, I am going.*

Then Adams said, "But, I am not going to send you. I hope you understand. You had a great year. Thanks." I was not number one. In fact, I was not number nine. I might have been number 11 or number 19. But, I wasn't going to the Final Four. I don't remember who went. I didn't watch. I couldn't do it. I belonged, had done all that was necessary, was one of the highest recommended, and the one guy with a chance to pull the trigger and put me in didn't do it. I don't hold it against John Adams at all. He was doing his job. I had told him all along I did not want any favors. Only advance me to the point I deserve it. No more, no less. I must not have deserved it. I didn't go. Again. Or ever.

I have found my peace.

My kids couldn't care less if I worked the Final Four. Sure, we would have had fun and they would have been proud of old dad, but that would have been fleeting. I have proven myself to them over the years. We are bonded. It is all good. They love me for what I am and not for where or when I blew some stupid whistle.

My legacy is the role I serve with mine—the time I have put into parenting and being a strong father who supports them through the bad times and good, the person who will always have their back. I may not have reached a "Number One" title in college basketball officiating, but I've stayed number one with my kids as a faithful and loving father.

Maybe it is morbid, but it is how my mind works. I know what I want on my grave stone. "Here lies a decent man. A good husband, brother, friend, and a great dad. And, here lies a ballplayer." That says it all for me.

My legacy also includes being a long-term top college basketball official at the highest level, a great and accomplished administrator and husband, a good ball player in his day, and a great friend to so many.

It's my role as a father though that means the most to me, not that I didn't make the NCAA Final Four. My legacy with my kids is my purpose. That's the number one that matters to me.

I probably could have done a lot more with my life. I think I had enough ability to be a CEO of a big company, or the AD at Oklahoma or Duke. But that didn't happen, for whatever the reason, just like I did not make the Final Four. But I have been a championship-level dad, I know that. And, that is all that really, really matters to me.

Qualities within your life make you number one. How you act every day, the way you treat others, pick yourself up and dust yourself off when things don't work your way all contribute to a life well-lived. We can let numbers or ratings define us, or find those personal measures that mean more when it comes to what's most important about our lives. I found my personal market. We all must find our own. ■

Chapter 15 Lessons

1. There's only one "number one." The rest of us aren't. That doesn't make everyone else losers. It means we all must find the niche in our personal lives that gives us purpose and provides value to others. This is different for everyone, because each of us is unique.

2. If you let others define your success, you are set up for failure. Because so many artificial goals, statistics and numbers are used to judge others in the business or sports world, many of us feel the need to fight that competitive game to show we are important. Set your own qualitative markers. Life is not a numbers game.

3. Being Number Two, Number Three or Number 19 holds dignity. The person who gets the choice assignment or all the publicity isn't necessarily the happiest. Sometimes the game you officiate in the quarter-finals dwarfs the championship game, so the nineteenth best official got to have the most fun. Remember to savor that moment.

Rick Hartzell, 8 months

Rick Hartzell, first grade

Rick Hartzell, 1966

Bob and Rick Hartzell, 1967

Rick Hartzell, 1978

Rick Hartzell right, 1970

Rick's father, 1942   *Rick's mother, 1999*

Jody Hartzell, Michael Jordan, Rick Hartzell 1998

*In business suits from left to right: Rusty Herring, Rick
Hartzell, John Moreau ,1990*

Purdue's Cuonzo Martin is greeted by the fans as he tries to inbound the ball. That's Bucknell A.D. Rick Hartzell trying to keep play in order.

Purdue @ Penn State, 1991

Rick Hartzell, US Sports Festival,1995

Rick Hartzell ,1993

Clemson vs UNC, 3/12/95. Left to right: Frank Scagliotta, Rick Barnes, Dean Smith, Rick Hartzell

ACC Tournament officials ,1998

Rick Hartzell and Bill Kennedy, at Texas Tech, 2000

Hartzell with Bruce Pearl, 2004

Rick Hartzell, director of athletics for University of Northern Iowa, wins showmanship award at Governor's Steer Show at Iowa State Fair, 2002

Butler University, 2008

Rick Hartzell SMU 2004

Michigan State, 2008

Chapter 16
Continuous Learning

The day we decide to stop learning — and most often that is a cognitive and personal decision — is the day we start to decay and go backwards. Especially in this day and age, continuous learning is essential if we want to stay current and up-to-date and function at our highest level to the end of our days. There is always something new to learn. You can always grow. If you set out every day to learn something new, and have that as a definitive goal, then you are assured personal growth.

What could be more exciting than knowing that each day you are going to strive to learn something new, even something minor, that will change the way you behave or work or parent; or simply that you have something new in your brain that you did not have at the beginning of the day. That's being alive.

In the basketball officiating business, like any other, continuous learning is crucial. The only way you get better at officiating is to be around and work with people who are better than you are. If they are willing to give and share their knowledge, then what you pick up enhances your learning curve at warp speed. If, and I emphasize IF, you are willing to listen and learn and apply the lessons and information you are taught.

After games are over, it is typical for referees to look at the most veteran guy in the crew and say "what do you have for me, what can I do to get better?" I often take that comment with a grain of salt. Does the younger and less experienced official really want to know what I think or does he just want me to tell him how great I think he is?

I'm from Iowa, where people are generally very honest and straightforward. I try to be that way — don't beat around the bush, get right to whatever it is that needs to be said, no sugar coating. One night after a game at Kansas State, I was riding home to Iowa with a young official who was trying to make it, to crack the level where you get a lot of games, are trusted by your supervisor. He asked me the dreaded question, "What do you have for me?"

I thought for a minute and then said, "Do you remember the play when you came from the half court line and took that little push on the rebound in front of me and our other partner?" He replied to me, "Yeah, I do, it had to be called."

With my temperature rising, I responded, "Don't you think the two of us, both veteran guys, who have been around for a long time, would have called that play had it needed to be called?" It was a first-half play, the younger partner came from a mile away to take it, broke the cardinal rule of staying in his primary spot to work his plays, and subsequently suffered the wrath of a veteran coach and the disdain from his senior partners.

My point to him was simple: All he could do was hurt himself with everyone involved by coming to take that play. The bump and foul was minor, it was a clear "play on." It was not a Division I college basketball foul. Both senior officials had passed on the play.

WHISTLE IN A HAYSTACK

If he wanted to improve and make it in the business, it was a play he had to lay off, wait, trust us to get if it needed to be called. He did not want to hear my input. He did not really want to learn. He wanted me to tell him how great he was. I couldn't do it, and had to be honest. Do you really want to improve or not? Do you really want my input? It was a very quiet ride home after that. Too bad. The guy could have been good. But he wouldn't listen to me or anyone else. Ever. No continuous learning there.

I have referenced Fred Barakat earlier in this book, calling him an excellent supervisor in the ACC — a tough guy, all business. Every year he would have the veteran officials come to Pittsburgh for the famed Five Star Basketball Camp, run by the legendary Howard Garfinkel. Nearly every good young coach and player got their start at that camp. And, since the camp was held during the college open-recruiting period, every name college coach was in attendance. Over 100 campers came to officiate and learn, and a dozen or so of the veteran ACC staff would critique their work. The games were played outside, down in a bowl-type setting, where the temperatures would be unbearable on a good day.

Barakat knew several things: 1) You learn by teaching others; 2) the camp staff would build a great camaraderie under these circumstances; 3) the college coaches who saw officials working so hard during the summer to improve and help others immediately gained respect for them; 4) officials learned in an "in-service" setting.

He was right on all points. We were doing some of the best continuous learning I have ever been involved with in regard to officiating. We would watch others work, help them, critique what went on and then discuss the plays we saw with each other after hours. It was hard work, but great fun and very, very valuable.

When I ran staff meetings in my administrative work, I would always try to end the meetings by having a 10-minute session where we would go around the room and let everyone tell us what they were doing in their work that was outside the norm, extra, special, unusual, or things no one knew about. Then, I would always let people expound on what they learned during the process of doing something unique. That way, everyone could learn from the good or the bad that the particular staff person had encountered.

One of the things that I have done in my life that I consider outside the norm is run a dirt race car team. Both my son Nate and my wife Jill drove cars that we owned over the years. They had a super late-model team and a spec motor car and an asphalt car and raced locally and around the country. It was an enormous amount of work. I called it crazy fun, but very challenging.

We had less resources and knowledge, but our equipment was good. If you did not try to pick up something new or keep up with the learning curve every day, then you had no chance to be competitive. I saw some of the brightest and most innovative people you could ever meet at the race track. They knew what they wanted and that was to go fast, have the car handle properly and get to the front of the pack. That's where you get paid, at the front at the end of the night. At the end of each night, we would look at each other and say, 'What did we learn tonight?' And, we kept a book of all the things we did and learned that helped us go faster, do better, be more competitive. If we did not try to continuously learn, we had no chance at all to be competitive.

My sister, Jody, is one of the greatest people God ever put on this earth. She and I had great parents (Bob and Neva) and they taught us to live and act the right way. We had love in our house. We grew up on a farm in north central Iowa and our world was small. But, it was awesome.

Jody is successful, positive and popular. And, she is a great mom and wife. She runs the Adult Education division for a local community college. I have watched her develop programs for area businesses that helped them immeasurably in terms of continuous adult learning. She runs seminars and lectures on all sorts of topics, some of them a bit crazy to be honest, but many of them just what the businesses and people of her region need to stay current and up-to-date and to learn things that are going on all over the world, so they and their business can stay on top of things and be better and more profitable. I see the satisfaction she gets out of delivering these services to the people of north Iowa. And, I am proud of her. She has helped me in so many ways, particularly the need to continuously learn.

I consider the greatest story of my life as one from my mother, a story I expect to stay with me the rest of my life: My mom was a character. She had her ear pierced seven times and wore little fake diamonds in the piercings. She wore orange capri pants and tennis shoes that lit up when she walked. She used to send me her bowling scores out of the newspaper, anonymously, not with a note or anything, just her scores, highlighted. She worked hard her whole life. She buried two husbands. Oh, and she beat cancer twice.

When I moved back to Iowa in 1999, one of the things that most excited me was getting to be with my mother more. She was in great health, she ran and walked every day, and she was only going to be 90 minutes away. We would get to spend the last years of her life together and have fun. She, along with my sister and her husband, helped me move in to my house in Cedar Falls. In that process, I told my sister that I thought something was wrong with mom. She didn't seem sharp like usual and she was a little low on energy, which was never the case.

My sister took our mom to the doctor to get tested and found she had cancer, again, for the third time. It was a brain tumor this time, the same thing that took our dad when I was 19 years old. It didn't seem right to me, but I was convinced that the only way I could help my mom was to convince her to fight the cancer — get the treatments that were recommended, do everything possible to beat this dreaded disease again.

"Fight." That was our word, she was going to fight this cancer and beat it. I promised to help her, and she promised to fight.

At first, her efforts and the treatments were promising. There was a chance. Jody did everything she could to help their mom. But, about Thanksgiving, after three months of dealing with the disease, it became obvious that the cancer was going to win.

We had a good Thanksgiving and Christmas was okay, but she was going downhill. Every day, I called her and we talked. We laughed. And, we stayed with our theme, she was going to fight. In the middle of January we put mom in hospice in Mason City, Iowa. I went to see her virtually every day, making the 90-minute trip each way, hoping to see some progress. And, wiping away the tears on the way home. She was still fighting, but slipping.

I went up to see her one night, when she hadn't spoken now for a few days. It was obvious that the end was near. I stood and talked to her even though I knew she couldn't hear me. I spent an hour just holding this wonderful woman's hand and looking at her, wishing I could do something to help her. I finally decided to leave, knowing I would be back tomorrow. As I walked out of the room, I heard my name.

It was mom, calling to me. I immediately went back to her, and put my head by hers. I swear to you, she said to me, "If you will just let me rest for a little while I will start to fight again." You can imagine how that made me feel. On her death bed she had just taught me the greatest lesson of my life. Keep fighting. Never give up or give in. Stay committed to your plan. Try hard to the very end. We lost my mom at the end of January of 2000. I still miss her every day. But, she left me with a lesson and a legacy that I will never, ever let get away from me. She taught me, she was my role model, she was my teacher, all the way to the end of her life.

Continuous Learning Addendum from Rick:

When I set out to write this book, I knew I would learn some new things. I had a lot of material, but I wasn't sure how to use it. Thank goodness for Dave Simon. He has propelled my continuous learning curve immensely. What I have learned the most in this process has been helpful to me in many ways in my life; you can do almost anything within reason if you set your mind to it; your memory is better than you think and you can get your brain activated to bring back a whole lot of information (some of it is even worthwhile); writing in the middle of the night is great therapy; and, most importantly, that I have been a very lucky and blessed person in my life. I was raised right. I have been around great people. I have accomplished some things, more than I probably deserved, and that as a person I am a decent human being with some talent, something I was never sure of in life. That continuous learning has been well worth the effort to me. ■

Chapter 16 Lessons

1. Never stop learning. As long as you breathe, you can learn.

2. Learning will come at you from many directions. Don't turn down appropriate feedback. Listen, pay attention, seek out other's opinions to help you grow. You'll be a better person for it.

3. Learn by teaching. One of the best ways to improve or master a skill is to teach others. By talking through and explaining the intricacies of what you know, you find that you continue to develop through this process.

Chapter 17
Leadership

Volumes of books and articles have been written on leadership. People have made a career out of talking, lecturing on and writing about leadership. I don't pretend to be an expert on leadership but I have been in many leadership positions as a coach, administrator, lead referee and parent. All of these jobs require some level of leadership. I kept notes on what worked for me in leadership positions and have been asked to speak and write about leadership on many occasions. And, as a parent for the past 33 years, I feel I've been in the most crucial leadership position of all, that of being a parent, for long enough to know what good-great leadership looks and feels like.

Here are "Hartzell's Keys to Leadership," compiled from over the years of experiences and many leadership opportunities:

1. People do not care how much you know until you show them how much you care.

2. The best leaders put themselves in the shoes they are trying to lead and ask themselves how they would like to be led if

you were them.

3. Leadership is simply the practice of "influence." As a leader it is your job to influence those whom you are trying to lead to do things the right way, every time.

4. Preach and practice family first.

5. More can be accomplished if credit for successes are spread among the team.

6. The best motivation comes from positive reinforcement that is fostered in a positive atmosphere of teamwork.

7. Fear of the leader does not motivate many people.

8. Respect for the leader will motivate most people.

9. Love and respect for the leader will motivate almost everyone.

10. In most cases, a sense of value to the group will outweigh all other factors. Salary is always important, but it is often not the single most important factor.

11. Great communication, and thus, leadership, requires face-to-face, eye contact, one-on-one listening and discussion.

12. Great leaders are great listeners. They listen, think, re-think, and then respond.

13. In order to lead, you must have your boots on the ground. You must be out in the trenches and be visible.

14. As a leader, you cannot be afraid to be uncomfortable at times.

15. As a leader, you must be comfortable being a role model. Whether you like it or not, the people you lead watch your re-action, your behavior and what you do and say. "Actions speak louder than words" has to be the mantra of any great leader.

16. A great leader sets the agenda, sets the atmosphere, clearly

describes and communicates the expectations and then gets out of the way and allows everyone to do what they are supposed to do. Then, that performance or behavior is quickly assessed and discussed and positive feedback is given first, followed by any necessary corrective action, gently delivered.

17. The leader must be the ultimate team player.

18. At least some of the time the leader needs to be the first to arrive and the last to go.

19. The leader needs to "expect to be exceptional."

20. In almost every circumstance the leader must set the tone for "outperforming the available resources."

21. Every great leader must convince those he or she is leading that every person has within themselves an inexhaustible reserve of potential that they have never even come close to realizing. Great leadership will get them headed down that path.

22. The great leader needs to re-set the agenda or plan periodically. Rearrange the furniture. The greatest of successes you will ever attain are still waiting for you on the road ahead.

Hartzell Leadership Quotes:

"Approach every day of your work life like it is your first day, and every day with your family like it is your last day.

"What lies ahead of you and what lies behind you are minor compared to what lies inside of you.

"Things turn out best for people who make the best out of the way things turn out.

"Do the events of your life define or refine you?

"Guide that which goes off the road, and love people who are the least lovable because they need the love the most.

"The measure of success is not whether you have a tough problem to deal with but rather whether it is the same problem you had last year.

"Your job as a leader is to keep the rapidly moving truck between the guard rails and on the road, even though it might swerve around a bit." ■

Chapter 18
Building Your Best Team

I believe that every one of us wants to be a part of a successful team of some sort. We start our lives wanting to be part of athletic teams, or a team at church or the Cub Scouts or Girl Scouts. Associating with a successful group of other people is something the human spirit desires and seeks.

That is why so many people are fans of a professional or college team to which they really have no particular affiliation. That is why there are senior level bowling leagues, softball teams, dart leagues, or any other team bonding experience — to share a passion, to care so much about something that it makes you get out of bed with a spring in your step.

Team experiences give you something to look forward to each day. I go to a church in my town that is truly a family and a team of people. People are happy, they smile and greet each other. It is a social gathering, an event, and worship every Sunday. There is energy and synergy and excitement. The church is filled for three services every weekend plus Wednesday night youth programs.

There is no doubt in my mind that while the church is great, the staff is awesome and the message wonderful, that part of the reason the place is so popular is because people are made to feel a part of the greater good there and they have a team to play on.

I have been a part of teams of some sort for most of my life. I played all the sports. I was part of groups of people that performed like teams do. I managed athletic programs with one goal in mind — to build the best possible team of people that I could in order to do the work the best that it could be done.

One of my most vivid memories and life-changing moments came as a freshman football player at UNI. We were gathered for our first team meeting and handed our playbooks. The first page of the playbook was a list of team rules. Number one was this: You are not all equal and you all will not be treated equally. I was shocked by that statement and not at all sure what it meant. Where I came from and how I was raised we were all equal and would be treated equally. But I quickly came to realize what the statement meant. If you had more talent or value to the process of building the team, you got some special treatment. After a few days, it was clear that I was not at the top of the depth chart. I had some talent, but my lifelong bugaboo got me — I did not run well enough. So, the guy at the top of the depth chart at my position, quarterback and then tight end, got treated a lot differently than I did. It was okay, I understood. My coach was interested in building a team and teaching life's lessons, and he got through to me in a hurry.

"A rising tide raises all the boats" was a saying that I have used many times. We built some great programs at Northern Iowa while I was there because of the excellent people on staff and those we hired. We had a great blend of veterans and youth. We had some programs that were really good and some that were trying to be really good.

One of the programs of national caliber during my tenure was women's volleyball. I hired a coach at UNI named Bobbi Peterson. She had a tremendous playing career at UNI and then took over the program. I worked hard with Bobbi to help her develop the best possible program. Why?

The body of people who care about women's volleyball was smaller than that of football or men's basketball. Why spend that time and effort on women's volleyball? Because we had a niche. We had a program that had been successful and we thought we could take it to a national level. We thought that if we could do it in women's volleyball, then the bar would be raised for everyone else, all other programs.

The coaches, fans and student-athletes would be inherently pushed to accomplish more in their program and try to match the volleyball success. We did it in track and field with a fabulous coach in Chris Bucknam. We did it in football. We did it in men's basketball with Greg McDermott and then Ben Jacobsen. We did it women's basketball with Tony DiCecco and then Tonya Warren. And baseball with Rick Heller. And on and on. We built a great team of teams and of people. And everyone was better for it. The rising tide of volleyball raised all the boats. And everyone, the community, our campus, fans, and all the people who rose to the challenge of being a part of the best team around were all better for it.

How do you build your best team? Here are my tips:

1. Make a championship level effort, every day

2. Surround yourself with talented and supportive people

3. Be a team player yourself and accept your role

4. Out-perform your resources

5. Be a great communicator

6. Be positive

7. It is "we" not "I"

8. Recognize the power of great chemistry opposed to great talent

9. Empower and inspire others

10. Grow from learning the best qualities of others on your team

11. Your work ethic must be unquenchable

12. A positive and upbeat atmosphere is critical to success. YES WE CAN!

13. Have a true passion for the mission

14. Have fun — enjoy, smile, spread the joy

15. Have the sense of a goose!

My reference in number 15 above is important. This fall, when you see geese flying along in a "V" formation that we so often see, think about the reason they fly that way. They are a part of a team, making a cross-country pilgrimage. As each goose drafts the one in front of them, the whole flock adds 65 percent more flying range than if they were flying alone. (People who are a part of a great team and sense of community are much more successful). When one goose falls out of formation and tries to go it alone, it suddenly feels the drag and it gets back into formation to take advantage of the lifting power of the bird directly in front of it. When the lead goose gets tired, it rotates back in the formation and another goose takes the point. The geese honk from behind in the formation to encourage those who are leading. When a goose gets sick or falls out of the formation, two geese will always follow him to protect and help. They stay with him until he is better and then they set out, as a group to launch their own team or to find another group to join.

If we have the sense of a goose, then these ideas can help us in our daily lives and in our lives as team members, leaders or developers.

The reason that so few teams or individuals get great is because they get GOOD and then they stop. They think good is enough. They get satisfied and they know it all. This mentality moves the team from growth to maintenance. Ask yourself, how far can you go to make yourself and your team better? How good can you or your team be? Can you use your success as a stepping stone to better and not a pedestal? Can you do the right thing, can you make the right call at the precise time? Do not limit yourself. Be a part of the best team you can surround yourself with and then flourish personally.

It is absolutely crucial for all of us, no matter what our profession or avocation, to have an unbreakable bond with someone. That might be a spouse or a friend. It might be a teammate from one of the teams of which you are a part. It might be a neutral third party who will tell it like it is directly to you. But, you must have someone whom you can count on in good times and bad to support you, celebrate with you, commiserate with you, pick you up when you are down, or just talk straight to you when you need some solid advice.

I have worked for some brilliant people in my life. One of the things that I've found is that the smartest people can take the most complicated issues and simplify them into a small set of "to dos" that will let you move forward and find solutions.

That's what great team members do for each other. That is what the person with an unbreakable bond will do for you. No matter what mistake you make or what error in judgment you have, they will be there. They will not judge you. They will not talk down to you. They will work with you and support you and go any extra distance necessary to help you at any time of any day, 24/7/365, forever and always. I am so fortunate to have a few people like that in my life. And, I know it has helped me immeasurably to have some success in life.

Being a part of an uplifting team is critically important. Surround yourself with people who will give you energy and excitement. Do not surround yourself with those who suck that energy out of you. Let's face it, some people, as well-being as they might think they are, are really toxic to us; they take away our energy or our will due to their negativity or their personal issues or idiosyncrasies. Do not let them do it. Be a part of a successful team so that you can become the very best that you can be.

My Team Tips:

- GET AWAY FROM THE PEOPLE IN YOUR LIFE WHO SPEND THEIR TIME TELLING YOU WHAT IT IS THAT YOU CAN'T DO

- LIFE'S CURRENCY IS THE FRIENDS WE MAKE

- THERE IS NOTHING THAT YOU AND I, TOGETHER, CANNOT OVERCOME TODAY

- BY YOUR OWN SOUL, LEARN TO LIVE; AND IF MAN THWART YOU, PAY NO HEED; IF MAN HATES YOU, HAVE NO CARE; SING YOUR SONG, DREAM YOUR DREAM, PRAY YOUR PRAYER; BY YOUR OWN, SOUL LEARN TO LIVE ■

Chapter 19
Physical Conditioning

One of the saddest things in the world I see is when people get older, perhaps when they've reached retirement age, after having worked hard for a lifetime, they become physically unable to enjoy their golden years. They have let their personal physical conditioning go to the point that they cannot move or enjoy themselves. I see it every day, nearly everywhere I look — people who don't even attempt to take care of themselves. After years of neglect, they pay the price.

It is sad to me. People should be able to enjoy their days on this earth as much as possible because time is fleeting. And, nearly all of these people have families and friends who love and care for them so much and want to spend all the time with them they possibly can.

All of us have little physical issues as we age. My mom used to tell me, "getting old is not for sissies." And, of course, she was right. No one can escape the rampage of Father Time. However, nearly all of us know that diet and exercise are crucial to our long-term well-being and quality of life. For some of us, it is a daily battle.

I have probably gained and lost 2,000 pounds in my lifetime. I battle weight every day and have to think about it and work on it constantly. If I look at a cookie or some sweets, I can gain weight. I'm at my best at about 205 pounds, but range from 200 to 220. I work out every single day, biking, running, swimming, taking kick boxing classes, and lifting weights.

Imagine what I would look like if I didn't! And, I like the workouts. I enjoy the sweat and the effort and know that I have to do it if I want to have the good quality of life.

If l stop my workout regime for two or three days, I feel miserable. I'm unhappy with how I feel physically and mentally. I like pizza, diet soda, brownies and chocolate chip cookies, and consume them in moderation, most of the time. But nothing deters me from doing everything I can to try my best to stay in a physical conditioning state where I can do what I want when I want, without being so stiff and sore I cannot get out of bed.

When I speak to young people in schools or camps, I always stress the importance of trying to maintain physical conditioning or doing something physical every day with an eye on their future. Once you lose the battle, it is hard to start over and get back into the shape you want or need to be to fully function. I make a similar point about mental acuity — each of us needs to do something every day to stay sharp, to keep our memories and brains functioning at as high a level as we can for as long as we can. The alternative, of which all of us are aware, is very, very difficult.

Motivation to stay in great physical condition is generally the issue. People are busy with work, hobbies, families, and other important obligations. But there are some key things to think about as we try to motivate ourselves to get up off the couch and do what is necessary to get or keep ourselves in appropriate physical condition. For example:

1. Get up, get out and do something physical each day, no matter how minor.

2. Make realistic and reachable goals.

3. If we are going to lose weight, it is simple — we need to burn more calories than we take in. There is no magic pill or formula. That is it. Eat less, work more.

4. Jump back on the wagon immediately if you fall off. Get back at it.

5. Eat better, smarter, less.

6. Establish a plan and try hard to stick with it.

7. If you fail at your plan, do not beat yourself up; pick yourself up and start again.

8. Think often about the positives that come from working out — flexibility, decreased appetite, personal pride in accomplishment. Hang on to that high that you get from the work.

9. Drink more water. More than half the population is dehydrated. Drinking more water helps you in many ways.

10. Find a partner, a mentor or someone who will push you to do better and not to quit. All the popular workout programs encourage this partnership as a way to stay motivated.

A commitment to physical fitness means making it one of the most important things you do every day. Fitness must become a habit, a rhythm of your life that makes missing a day or two something that bothers you to the point where you commit to not letting it happen frequently.

Bad habits are acquired through repeated bad acts. Habit is overcome by habit. By working on good habits we can slowly replace our bad ones. We all feel better about ourselves if we stay with our resolutions for change, for doing things that make us better. There is no doubt, and it is impossible to argue, that a commitment to fitness is one of the best things that we can do for ourselves and for those who care about us.

I have referenced my mother in this book previously. She was truly one of a kind. She was loving and kind, yet tough and strong. She was a great wife. She could cook like no one else, even though she downplayed that skill in her 'Iowa way.' She became committed to her physical fitness a bit later in life, like many in her generation. She ran or walked every day. One day she was leaving her house in the dead of winter to do her 2.5 mile walk/run route around the town she lived in, Garner, Iowa. She slipped going down Main Street in Garner, and broke her wrist. But, she continued on her run, knowing she was hurt. When she got home, she called my sister to tell her about her fall. She got her wrist fixed, but she did not miss her run.

This is the same woman who ran/walked in some 5k races. Of course, she was all about trying to win her age group. But there was always one woman who was a year older than mom who she couldn't beat. I will never forget her joy when that woman finally moved up an age group for a year and then mom had the chance to win her age group. She liked that medal a lot. If I re-call correctly, that is also the year that she passed my sister late in the race and made farting noises under her arm as she passed Jody. You can see why we miss her. She was the life of the party. And, her commitment to her physical fitness allowed her to have a high quality of life all the way to the end of her days.

There are a lot of reasons and excuses that we all can make not to exercise on a daily basis. Some of these are legitimate — a family or work crisis, an injury. But many times we allow ourselves an out when it comes to important things that we need to do.

Other than your family and your faith, it seems to me that nothing is more important than your personal health and physical conditioning. There is no time like the present to start making some progress in that area of our lives. We will all be better for that effort.

My observations on conditioning:

- Enjoy a lifetime of movement so you can enjoy movement for a lifetime!

- What I am is God's gift to me...what I make of myself is my gift to Him.

- Great people are just ordinary people with an extraordinary amount of determination.

- It is a whole lot better to wear out than to rust.

12 THINGS SUCCESSFUL PEOPLE DO DIFFERENTLY FROM OTHERS

1. They create and pursue goals.
2. The take immediate and decisive action.
3. They focus on being productive, not being busy.
4. They make logical and informed decisions.
5. They avoid the trap of trying to make everything perfect.
6. They work outside their comfort zone.
7. They keep things simple.
8. They focus on making small, continuous improvements
9. They measure their progress.

10. They maintain a positive outlook as they learn from their mistakes.

11. They spend their time with the right people.

12. They maintain balance in their life. ■

Chapter 20

Ref a Season – A joint closing message from Rick Hartzell and Dave Simon

When we started putting together this book, we outlined many of the chapters, pulling together notes from both of us. We didn't know the title at the outset or how many chapters would evolve. We did agree though that a final chapter encouraging everyone to officiate a sport for a season would be an ideal closer. Here's why.

The life lessons from *Whistle in a Haystack* go far beyond the basketball court. Both of us have grown in many ways, often unexpectedly, based on our officiating experiences. That's what led to this book.

But more than that, officiating molded us into better human beings. It taught us how to enforce rules, mentor others, accept direct and often painful feedback from irate parents, coaches and fans, recognize we weren't going to be number one (or if we were, that standing would be fleeting), and admit our mistakes then move on.

We understand and handle conflict better today than years ago before we put on the striped shirt. We developed techniques to listen closely to angry people, acknowledge their concerns, and demonstrate we understand what bothers them. Those are good qualities to develop as a human being, and we believe strongly the officiating basketball helped us immensely down that path.

Because of our experiences, we want to suggest a seemingly weird idea, but one we believe can help improve the way people relate to each other and understand differing perspectives, while cultivating an appreciation on the need for rules and enforcement in modern societies. We recommend that everyone officiate a sport for an entire season. If you love basketball, give it a try. If football is your thing, get out on the field. If you're a big soccer fan, sign up with your local association.

Officiating will push you out of your comfort zone. You will learn new things. You will grow in your understanding of the sport and as a person. You will diffuse conflict (or you won't survive).

It seems a lot of these qualities are more and more necessary in today's conflict-driven world, and less and less in supply. We yell at each other. People whine, complain and point fingers. "It's the ref's fault." You rarely hear, "It's my fault." It's hard to find people seeking the blame for something not working out in business, politics or in a sporting event.

As an official, you cannot hide from your mistakes. They are there for everyone to see, and as we have pointed out on these pages, you must move on from them. That's another skill you would develop in your season of officiating a sport.

World peace may seem an odd thing to bring up at this stage of the book, but if everyone in the U.S., or indeed, even the world, accepted the challenge to officiate a sport for a season, we believe a goal for a more peaceful world is closer to our grasp. Humans are too complex to expect all conflicts to go away. But we can manage them much better, employing dignity, better listening skills and a willingness to recognize two sides (teams) on an issue. That's the beauty of the sports arena: Both teams want an advantage. They will (at times or perhaps even frequently or deliberately) seek to break the rules. As an official, you will develop a new faith in enforcing the rules on the books. Otherwise there is chaos. Those skills and tactics go a long way towards making you a better businessperson, husband or wife, or even a negotiator with a foreign country on a peace treaty.

Sports officials are like police officers and judges rolled into one. You find this out quickly. People lie to you about what happened on the court. "Man, I never touched him." "That ball went off him." Sometimes they are small lies and other times deliberate attempts to manipulate you. As the officer and judge on the court, you have to develop an intuitive sense of what drives people — their emotions and motives — while ensuring fairness, equity and enforcement of the rules. It is not easy. We salute any person who puts on a uniform to maintain a just and moral society. Too many seek to circumvent it. Your year on the court or field would give you a much deeper appreciation of our law enforcement officers and the judges who must rule on our laws.

We recommend you officiate one season. But if we've been successful with this book, we hope officiating jazzes you up and you come back for a second and a third. If you get that far, you're probably hooked on the sport. You can take it wherever you want — middle school, recreation league games, high school, perhaps even college or the pros with dedication, hard work, and a honed skill level.

Find your *Whistle in a Haystack* and head down to your local association. Get on the internet. Talk to someone in your hometown who you see on the court or field. Figure out where to sign up. A fraternity of others who care about the game is waiting for you. Get started.

If you decide that you just can't take our urging and start to officiate, make a pledge to at least consider this request: be gentle and considerate and less critical of those who do officiate all the games that you watch. Regardless of the level of the game, from Little League to NFL football, the men and women officiating these games are your neighbors, your friends, someone's mom or dad. They are trying their very best to get every play right, to give both teams an equal chance to win and to do it with the highest level of professionalism possible.

Officiating is not easy. Mistakes are made. But, I have never met an official, at any level, in any type of game, who "missed a play in their heart." In other words, officials do not miss plays on purpose. They do not try to favor one team or another. They do not try and make people mad and create controversy. It is just not in their DNA. They do not try and call fouls just on the team you are cheering for; they do not call a strike a ball just for spite; they don't call holding just because they feel like it. I heard a coach sarcastically say one time that what is wrong with officials is that "they just don't care who wins." And, that is the truth. They do not care who wins. Fans care. Parents and grandparents and alumni and boosters and coaches care about who wins. Officials do not. They care about getting plays right. That is it. Nothing more, nothing less.

Think about this for a minute: what would it be like to have a hundred or a thousand or ten thousand or a hundred thousand people looking over your shoulder and watching and scrutinizing your every move at your job. When you made a mistake in your work (and everyone makes a mistake now and then) what would you do if all those people yelled and cursed and booed, and called you names? It would be very hard to do your work under those circumstances. I am not asking you not to get excited or upset over a poor call by any official. As a fan that is your right to do. But, I would ask that you remember that the man or woman out there officiating does not want to make a mistake, they want to be right on every call. They have all sorts of people to whom they report who are watching the game, reviewing their every move and call, replaying the video in super-slow motion and filing a report on their work. Have a little compassion for them.

Understand that something might have happened that could have caused them to make a mistake, a bad call. Maybe a player stepped right in front of them at just the most critical moment and they could not see the play. Maybe the catcher stood up or moved and what was a strike looked like a ball. Maybe the defender wrapped his arm around the wide receiver on the back side of the receiver where the official couldn't see perfectly. Maybe a player just barely tipped the ball on the way out of bounds and no one could see it. Things happen. Things happen in every game that are just inexplicable. How could that possibly happen? Hard to explain, but they do.

And, the last thing for your consideration in this regard: players drop passes, miss layups, swing and miss at a pitch right down the middle or throw wildly errant passes. Coaches put their teams in the wrong defense, or make poor substitutions or do not manage the clock correctly. It happens in every single game. So, please have some compassion and understanding for that official, for that referee or umpire who is out there working hard in the games you watch. Don't curse them in public. Don't call them bad names. Don't set a bad example for all those around you to think it is okay to say whatever words that come to your mind about the character of the man or woman making the call. Have some restraint, some understanding, and be reasonable. Be human and be humane. **Because, I can guarantee you this: they did not miss the play in their heart.** ■

YOU HAVE TO KNOW AND UNDERSTAND THESE THINGS IF YOU ARE EVER GOING TO REFEREE BASKETBALL AT A HIGH LEVEL

1. YOU ARE STARTING A JOURNEY
2. This business (and it is a business) is all about building credibility.
3. You must work a lot of games for virtually no money before you can make it to the point where you can work a lot of games for a whole bunch of money.
4. They never, ever "boo" you at the bank.
5. You only get better by working with people who are better than you.
6. If you are good enough, if you get calls right and you manage games right, then you will advance.
7. Know the rules. Know the right mechanics. Stay in shape. You can control these things.
8. Position. Position. Position. Nothing else matters if you do not know what this means.
9. Blow the whistle when you "KNOW" you are right. And stay in your primary area.
10. Be the greatest partner you can possibly be. Have everyone love to see your name on the line.
11. They will continue to play the games when you are long gone. For sure.
12. Referee today's game and referee it like it is the most important game in the world to someone.
13. If you think having coaches like you will help you advance, you are very, very, wrong.
14. Be confident. Do not be arrogant. There is a huge difference.
15. Be FIRM BUT FRIENDLY.

16. Priorities: Family. Faith. Friends. Vocation. Avocation.
17. To make it you will have to go to big-time camps. Probably many times. Pay the price.
18. Have a plan. Evaluate your plan and your weaknesses. Reload.
19. Keep a game by game list of the things that you learn or need to do better. Journal.
20. You cannot do this at a high level if you cannot THINK on your feet.
21. Limit your words in every setting. Silence cannot be quoted. Have "go to" words.
22. Get a mentor. Have an unbreakable bond. Have someone who loves you even when you have a horrible night. It is the only way you will survive. Because you will have horrible nights.
23. Your perfect game: come in the back door; work the game; give your best effort; leave through the same door. Get paid. Be absolutely unnoticed. That is the perfect game and yourself.
24. Once the ball is tipped off do not ever "shut down" or completely relax. Do not be surprised by plays, actions/reactions of coaches or players. You must manage the game.
25. Every game has a point in time where it needs a whistle or certain call to be made. When you are really good you will know exactly when that time has come and what the call should be.
26. Put a certain amount of each game check in a place where you cannot touch it. And, someday, you will have a big pile of money just from blowing a stupid whistle.
27. Treat your supervisors with respect, dignity and understanding. Use the "avenue of least resistance" as your guide.

28. IT IS NICE TO BE IMPORTANT. IT IS MORE IMPORTANT TO BE NICE.

29. When you are young and aspiring just call what is dead in front of you. Know the rules. Watch the clocks. Help when you can and let the guys that are really good handle the garbage. Learn. Remember. Do it again, and again. Soon you will be ready to assume a leadership position.

30. ENJOY THE JOURNEY.

The following is reprinted with the author's permission

Washington Post
January 1998

The Ref
By John Feinstein

It is halftime on a Sunday afternoon in January and the Atlantic Coast Conference basketball game between Virginia and Clemson is tight. Virginia, playing at home, is trying to break a six-game ACC losing streak. Clemson needs a victory to stay in the hunt for an NCAA tournament berth. The home team leads by four at the break, and, as you might expect, the locker rooms are tense.

Rick Hartzell sits in a chair, pops open a soda and looks at his teammates. "How do you guys think we should handle this?" he says. "I want to get things under control here before they get any worse."

Hartzell's uniform isn't Virginia home white or Clemson road orange. It is no-win black and white — the stripes of a referee. His concern at the moment has nothing to do with the outcome of the game. Late in the first half, Clemson Coach Larry Shyatt had "gone off." He had been hit with a technical foul by Curtis Shaw, who, along with Larry Rose, is working the game with Hartzell. Normally mild-mannered, Shyatt had been almost out of control when Hartzell came to the bench to try to calm him down.

"I don't care if it costs me my career," Shyatt had said. "I'm going out there and hit that guy."

The comment surprised and concerned Hartzell. He didn't really believe Shyatt was going to try to hit Shaw, but he didn't want the situation to deteriorate in the second half. One more technical and Shyatt would be ejected. Refs don't like to toss coaches unless they have to.

Hartzell, who in real life is the athletic director at Bucknell University, has been a college basketball official since 1982, He is 45, a farm boy from Iowa who says his hometown of Klemme has a population of 500, "on a good day." While he was coaching football and baseball at Coe College, he took an officiating class to see what officials go through. "I got hooked fast," he says. "I liked the idea of trying to do something well that's hard to do."

Refereeing, especially in the high-stakes, high-pressure ACC, is just that: hard to do. Hartzell can vouch for that. He is highly respected by coaches and an annual invitee to work the NCAA tournament in March. He works about 60 games a year (at $650 plus expenses per game), often racing back to his office for meetings, then hitting the road again. His schedule for five days in mid-January is typical: Florida State-Duke Saturday; Clemson-Virginia Sunday, office Monday morning, Wofford-VMI Monday night, office Tuesday, Wofford-North Carolina State Wednesday.

As good as Hartzell is, he has had setbacks: In 1989, working a regional semifinal in the NCAAs for the first time, he blew a critical call in the final minutes of a game between Georgetown and N.C. State, making a phantom travel call on a play that might have allowed N.C, State to tie the game. "I've never even looked at the tape," he says. "I know I blew it. I don't want to see it."

Eight years later in a game at Virginia, Hartzell failed to wave a substitute into a game with five seconds left and his mistake led to a tainted victory for Duke. It also led to the ACC suspending all three officials for one game and keeping Hartzell away from Virginia until early this season.

"Those kinds of screw-ups eat at you," Hartzell says "I think they've made me better, because I'm more focused, more determined to be as good as I possibly can be."

There is no discomfort for Hartzell working at Virginia. In fact, when Clemson sent a sub to the scorer's table late in the first half to come in for someone shooting a free throw—the identical situation that led to the debacle in '97 — Hartzell turned to time-keeper Cy Weaver and said, "Cy, we're going to get this sub in FOR SURE."

Now, a few minutes later, he has to make a much more serious decision: how to deal with Shyatt. One option is to do nothing and hope Shyatt calms down after the 15-minute halftime break. Another possibility is to call both coaches together for a chat. All coaches are absolutely paranoid about seeing an official talking to their counterpart. In the first half, when Shyatt began jawing at Shaw, Virginia Coach Pete Gillen had jumped off his bench and shrieked, "Work the game, Curtis, quit talking!"

Hartzell, who is the referee for the game and therefore in charge — the other two officials are technically called umpires — makes a decision. "I'll have a quiet word with Larry," he says. "I'll tell him he's too good a coach to jeopardize his future over one game, no matter what he thinks did or didn't happen, Then I'll go tell Pete exactly what I told him."

Shaw and Rose nod in agreement. There's a knock at the door. Time to go back to work. Hartzell speaks to both coaches. Shyatt says three words to Hartzell: "Thanks. I'm okay."

He is, but his team isn't. Virginia pulls the upset. For the offi-cials, there are no further problems. The crisis has been averted. A few minutes after the final buzzer, Shyatt pokes his head into the officials' locker room. Everyone stiffens for a moment. "I just came to apologize," he says. Everyone shakes hands. When Shyatt is gone, Hartzell turns to his partners and says, "That was a class thing to do." He smiles, "We all make mistakes."

The officials dress and head for their cars, wishing one another luck in the weeks to come As they are leaving, a security guard says, "Good job today, guys." Rick Hartzell laughs. "We hear that a lot," he says, "when the home team wins." ■

Referee Requiem
Additional Stories

(Editor's note: Not every story from the basketball court falls neatly into a chapter in a book. Here are a few more stories we felt worth sharing, for those of you who have gotten this far and want to enjoy the ride a bit longer.)

My first college refereeing partner and the guy who got me started in officiating was a dear friend (to this day), Joel Paige. We were friends in college and carried that forward in our adult lives. Joel got me started refereeing junior high and small high school games.

He was an excellent referee and a great baseball umpire, he just needed a break that he never got. We would go anywhere to officiate games when we started. We worked high school games for $27.50 a night, two games — girls game first and then the boys. Big money, man. By the way, in those days the girls' games were the old Iowa and Tennessee rules, six-on-six, half court. Quite a game, and the gyms were always full. You would work the girls' game in front of a full house and the boys' game would have a gym half full.

We also worked Division III men's games in our second year together. I will never forget how we felt getting to officiate college games. We drove all over the Midwest. Our first game was at Upper Iowa University in Fayette, Iowa, and we made $60. We were living large.

One night, Joel and I worked a junior college game in Burlington, Iowa, for one of the perennial junior college powers, Southeastern Community College, coached by a long-time and highly successful coach, Jim Wyatt. His teams were always good, and he was considered a character. On this night, his team played Kennedy King junior college out of Chicago. It was a great game, and Kennedy King beat Southeastern in front of a full house. In those days, the coaches booked their own officials so you can imagine that having the home team lose did not do much for your next year's officiating schedule.

But, Joel and I didn't care — work the game, do your best, give both teams a chance and hold your head high. We went to the locker room after the game and as we sat down to get dressed there was a knock on the door. I answered the door and it was Coach Wyatt. He looked at us both and said, "No one will ever say they get homered at Southeastern, that is for damn sure." And he shut the door. Joel and I looked at each other and smiled. It was the ultimate compliment. We were fair. The best team that night won the game. The home team lost. And, we were invited back to Burlington to work games many times after that. We got the officials ultimate compliment.

●●●●●

The days of making $27.50 for a doubleheader are over, thank goodness. The pay scale for officials has changed dramatically in recent years, at every level for all sports. Not only did I start at $27.50 for a boy/girl doubleheader, and $60 for a Division III men's game, but I worked the men's junior college national tournament in Hutchinson, Kansas, early in my career, a huge thrill and very good and difficult basketball to work. I got paid $550 total. I worked two games a day from Tuesday-Friday. I worked the national championship game on Saturday night in front of 6,000 people. I paid for my own gas, travel expenses and meals for the week. All for $550. And, I would do it again.

I had an old friend in the officiating business named Stan Rote, who lived in Baltimore. Stan was a funny, funny man. He could tell stories with the best of them. He used to say that if you told the normal person that there were two one hundred dollar bills underneath the welcome mat at the First Methodist Church in Buffalo, New York, and all they had to do to claim the money was go there and pick it up, that person would look at you like you were crazy. But, if you told an official that there was a game in Buffalo that paid $200 you would have a stampede to see who could go work that game. He was right on with that analogy. The pay has gotten better, much better in some cases, and that is a good thing for the officials. Along with that increase in pay has come a higher level of scrutiny and accountability as well, and that is good for everyone who plays, coaches or officiates. Demanding a better result in the calls that are made makes the games better for everyone involved.

• • • • •

Very early in my career, when officials still worked some two-man games in college basketball, I officiated the Eastern Illinois-Western Illinois game, a big rivalry game, in Macomb. I worked the game with a veteran official out of Chicago named Otho Kortz. They started the game fine. Suddenly, I saw Otho sitting on the court, so I stopped the game to see what was going on.

He looks at me and says, "Rick, someone shot me. They shot me right out of the stands. They shot me." I said, "Otho, where did they get you?" Otho replied, "Right in the leg I think, the back of my leg." I looked at Otho's leg, and it wasn't that he was shot (obviously) but that he had torn his Achilles tendon. So, I broke the news to him and the training staff helped him off the court.

We were down to one official.

I met with the coaches and told them I would do my best and work as hard as I could to get everyone through the game, and I did just that. I was younger, so I ran from end to end.

It was a great game that, if I remember right, Western Illinois won. As is usual, the coaches do a rating of the officials after the game and in a day or two you get that rating to see how you did, and what you can improve on in your game. The categories are usually appearance, demeanor, communication, rules knowledge, game management, hustle. Pretty standard stuff. The rating scale then was one for not acceptable and 10 for great work. I got all nines and 10's for this game with the exception of the coach at Western Illinois, Jack Mergenthaler, a real character, who gave me a one for hustle. I will never forget it. I worked a Division I game by myself, ran end to end, got through the game without any issues, got the calls right, and got a one for hustle.

•••••

When I lived in Chicago and worked at Northwestern University, I also officiated some junior college, high school, Catholic League and Division III games. It was hard for a country boy to get around in Chicago a lot of times given traffic, directions, no GPS, and no cell phone at that time. One night I was supposed to be at Kennedy King junior college which was near the old Chicago Stadium. I got lost — really lost — in the wrong part of town, a place where I knew I should not be. I didn't know what to do, it was approaching the time I needed to be in the gym.

I drove down a street and saw a man working on his car. I stopped and asked him for directions to Kennedy King. The man looked at me and said, "Man, what in the !@#$%^&*&^%$#@!

are you doing here?" I quickly told him I was refereeing the game at Kennedy King. He said, "Man I ain't never seen any white folk on this street. Follow me." He hopped on a bicycle and I followed him. He rode about two blocks and pointed east. I gave him $5 and got to the gym. I can still see his face. Thank you, man.

●●●●●

The two strong men in my life:

I have had two very strong men who were so very significant in my life. They both had a huge impact on me, and both guided my path from a boy to a man. The first was my dad, Bob Hartzell. My dad was a great man, a farmer, a World War II veteran, a gentle man. He cried (just like I do) at the simplest things. He was emotional, but loving and gentle. I honestly do not remember a single time when he missed one of my games or events, until he got sick. He was always there, always supportive and always my greatest fan. He taught me how to work hard; he taught me how to play right; and while he encouraged me, he never pushed too hard. You could not have a better dad than I had. He and my mom, Neva, were just the best. We grew up in a loving home.

Unfortunately, one night when I was 14 — and this memory is so vivid to me — my dad, during our "supper" as it is called in the Midwest, started eating his food with his hands. Out of the blue, no warning, he just started acting differently. He got headaches, he drove his truck in the ditch, and we all knew something was wrong. Come to find out, he had a brain tumor. We lived close to Rochester, Minnesota, and the Mayo Clinic, so we immediately went there. The news was not good, but they did operate and there was some optimism at first.

When I turned 16, I had my driver's license, and my mom was working to support the four of us, so I drove dad to his radiation treatments every day for a month, back and forth to Rochester. He slowly became worse and they operated again, but there was nothing they could do, the cancer was moving too fast. On a side note, my sister Jody and I had two parents in the same hospital, Mercy in Mason City, Iowa, at the very same time, two floors apart, at Christmas in 1970. Both had cancer. My mom would survive hers and live in great health until 2000. Dad died when I was 19-years-old and a sophomore at UNI. He did get to see me play football there a couple times and I know how proud he was of me, and of Jody too. No one should lose their parent that young. I have never forgotten my dad and never will. He was a great man.

The second major male figure in my life was my football coach at UNI, Stan Sheriff. While I was not a great player, nor necessarily one of his favorites, he took a liking to me. I became a graduate assistant for him at UNI in the football program and we spent a lot of time together looking at film, analyzing recruits and all the things that go along with coaching. He taught me so much, most of it good!

When I went off to do my college administrative work, Stan and I stayed in touch. He was busy and gruff and tough, but for some reason, he thought I was doing okay. We had breakfast in Nashville, at the NCAA convention on January 16, 1993. After breakfast he shook my hand and hugged me. At that time I was the AD at Bucknell University. Stan told me he was proud of me and gave me a handshake and a hug. When he flew home to Honolulu later that day, where he was the AD at Hawaii, his alma mater, he had a heart attack and died getting off the plane. Losing the two prominent male role models in my life is something that

WHISTLE IN A HAYSTACK

hurts. But, I took the best qualities of both of these men, and it has helped me make my way through life. I thank both of them from the bottom of my heart.

•••••

One of the hardest games in the country to work is Marshall vs. West Virginia. It is a huge rivalry in the state of West Virginia and always held in Charleston, WV. It's an almost impossible game to officiate, with hated rivals, and fans that are generally out of control. I officiated it a couple of times. One particular night, I had this game and was traveling to Charleston from my home and where I worked, in Lewisburg, PA. I got to the Williamsport, PA airport and my flight was cancelled. I had no choice but to take the three-hour drive to Dulles Airport in Washington, D.C., to make the last plane to Charleston to get to the gym at 5:30 p.m. as required, for a 7 p.m. game.

It was a 4 p.m. flight out of Dulles and it was 12:20 p.m. in Williamsport. I had to hurry, and thought I could make the plane but knew things had to go just right. I called United Airlines on the way and told them what was going on; they promised they had a seat for me. I drove to Dulles, called United again about 30 minutes out. No problem, they still held my seat. I parked the car, hustled to the gate as they started to board the plane.

Made it. Whew. I go to the counter and show the lady my boarding pass and she tells me that all the seats are taken, no seat for me. I try to remain calm, and explain the situation to her, but as travel goes sometimes, she is sorry, but no seat for me. We go through it all again, to no avail. This is a big deal to me. If I can't make the game, I don't get paid, I have to tell my supervisor about the issue, and in short, I am in trouble.

- 167 -

Before I gave up, I saw a young mother, probably 20-years old, go down the stairs to the plane. I asked the gate agent if the mom was using two seats, one for her and one for the very small baby she was carrying. The agent looked it up on the computer and yes, she had two seats. I asked the agent if there was any way that young mom could hold her baby and if I could have the other seat. She agreed to go ask. She came back with a wry smile on her face, so I was hopeful. I saw the young mom waiting before boarding the plane. The agent told me that the young mom would give me the baby's seat, but that I had to take care of the baby during the flight.

I was an experienced dad, and I had no other options, so I quickly agreed. I grabbed my bag, went down to the plane. The young mom looked at me. I explained that I was raising two young children and I could do this. She handed me the diaper bag and the baby. She said, "The baby's name is Abby. My name is Theresa. I am sitting in 3C. See you in Charleston." I made the game and Abby and I got along okay.

•••••

In February of 2005, I worked the Kansas State at Kansas game in Lawrence. This is one of the hard games each year, no matter where it is played. On this particular occasion, I was working with Dave Hall and Scott Thornley, two pros, good guys, great referees. I picked them up at the Kansas City airport Marriott and along with my wife Jill, we headed to Lawrence, about an hour from the airport. We were required to be in the locker room by 5:30 for a 7:00 game and we had plenty of time until we hit some traffic. We were running 15 minutes late and that is uncomfortable for referees. We were supposed to be there at 5:30. So, I was speeding to try and make up time. Sure enough, one of Kansas' finest policemen pulled me over. I handed him my license and registration. He asked, "Mr. Hartzell, where are you all headed in such a hurry?" I responded, honestly, "We are refereeing the basketball game at Lawrence tonight." He looked at my license again and then looked in the car and said, "You boys put on your hard hats tonight. You are going to need them. I will be watching. Go Wildcats." And he handed me back my license and went back to his car and drove off. Ticket avoided. A lobbying effort for the Kansas State Wildcats by a guy who understood what we were up against. Kansas beat Kansas State that night and I am sure the trooper watched the game. Sorry we couldn't bring the Wildcats home sir; we were just doing our jobs.

•••••

When I lived in Chicago, I got my first full-time appointment to a Division I staff, working in the Mid-American Conference. I was ecstatic. Bob Wortman was the supervisor who hired me, along with his permanent partners (how assignments were made back then) — a veteran named Dave Perry and another seasoned pro named Dick Bestor. Dave was from Michigan City, Indiana, and was an excellent football official who worked a Super Bowl and became the Big Ten supervisor of football officials. Bestor was from Fond du Lac, Wisconsin, and was a school principal.

It was a good gig for me — two veterans and a supervisor who trusted them at least, and me perhaps. He gave us a great schedule. I knew my job; be quiet, stay out of the way, learn, and do whatever Perry and Bestor told me to do. I could do that. I would meet Bestor on Ogden Avenue in Chicago and we would drive to the games. Actually, I would drive and he would sleep. He would drive the three hours to meet me, we would go to the game and referee, and I would drive him back to Ogden Avenue where he would then drive home to Wisconsin to be at school by 7:30 a.m. We did all of this for $225 a game each. Big time. But, a huge break for me and a way for Dick to continue his career.

On one particular night, the crew had a huge rivalry game — Ball State at Miami, Ohio. The schools are rivals to begin with, but in this year Ball State had added an Indiana transfer named Dan Palambizio, a big time player. Miami had the famous Ron Harper, who was an NBA great on the Chicago Bulls championship teams. It was an impossible game, hard from the start, and combative. Players growled, got physical, and no one backed down. Miami won in a very close and hard-fought game.

We had eight technical fouls, two ejections, probably 80 free throws. The game was not pretty. We got to the locker room after the game and I was certain my Mid-American officiating career had just ended before it really got started. The supervisor, the ever-tough Bob Wortman, came in the locker room after the game. Bob was a hard-nosed Big Ten and NFL official, worked the Super Bowl. My first job in the MAC was to count how many times Bob used the "F" word in our league officials meetings. I counted 144 times in three hours. He was a no BS guy.

He looked at the three of us for what felt like five minutes. He paced the locker room. He put on his coat and hat. Still nothing. I could sense Dave and Dick getting worried. It probably was 30 seconds total, but it seemed like forever. Then, he walked over to me first. Here it comes. You are fired. I was sure of it. Bob Wortman put out his hand looked me dead in the eye and said to me, "Great f---ing game, kid, you were f---ing awesome." I about fainted. He did the same for Dick and Dave. Then he left. We three adult men celebrated like we had won a championship. Which, in a way, we did.

•••••

Three seconds in the lane is a call referees hate to make. You only call it if you have to clean up play in the lane or if someone is in there so long that you do not have a choice. Fans love to call for three seconds, but they're the only ones obsessing over it. It gets called about two times a year per official who works college games, maybe less. You can talk players out of the lane most of the time and that is better than blowing the whistle, stopping play, turning the ball over and making everyone on offense, including the coach, mad.

One night at Maryland, I was working with an excellent official and friend, Zelton Steed. 'Z' was a good guy, and we meshed well. Z made a three-second ruling against Maryland early in the second half. On the following possession I had an offensive player for Towson (non-league game) drop dead in the lane. He caught the ball, dribbled in the lane, double-pumped. I had no choice — three seconds in the lane. It was okay because it balanced out the call Z just had at the other end. Consistency, you know.

We go back to the other end, and just as Maryland started their offense, Z calls another three seconds in the lane —three possessions in a row, three consecutive three-second in the lane violations. Our supervisor, Fred Barakat, was at the game so we knew there was going to be repercussions of some sort. I went to Z after the third one and said to him, "Z, we are probably in a little trouble here. Fred is going to think we were messing around again." Zelton said what I knew was true, "Fred always tells us to use the three-second call to clean up the lane. That's what we did'."

But, I noticed a little smile on Zelton's face. We got in the locker room after the game, which Maryland won, so no consequence on the extra three-second call on them. Fred came in and even he had a little smile on his face. He said, "We haven't had three three-second calls made all year in this league and you guys have three in a row, in three possessions. Unbelievable."

Nobody said anything. Sometimes it is just better to be quiet and see what happens next. Barakat put on his coat and headed for the door. He looked over his shoulder at the crew and grunted, but with just the hint of a smile on his face. That was it. I looked at Z.

"Well, I guess we set a record," I said.

No one has ever done that before. Crazy. I asked Gary Williams, the Maryland coach, about it a week or so later at another game. He just looked at me with that smile he had and said, "You guys are crazy." I took that as a compliment from Gary. He knew.

•••••

My greatest week in my athletic administrative history happened in 2002. While at UNI we beat Eastern Illinois in the first round of the football playoffs with Tony Romo as their quarterback; we beat Minnesota in the first round of the NCAA volleyball tournament after being down 2-0; we beat Arkansas in women's basketball and we upset Iowa in men's basketball in the UNI-Dome in front of 16,000 fans. It gets no better than that.

•••••

When you are out on the road officiating games night after night, the little things mean a lot. In Louisville, the police come to your hotel, pick you up and take you to the locker room, and then back to the hotel after the game.

Nice. (But I think they do it so they can get into the games for free.) At Georgetown, they always had toiletries and snacks laid out before the game; you could take whatever you wanted or needed. At TCU there is always a goodie bag of stuff for each official every night. At Texas Tech they bring in these individual pies that are made in Lubbock and are really good. And in many places you have to fight to get a towel to use after you shower.

•••••

I thought I was ready to work a big-time Division I schedule well before I really was ready, something that holds true for many officials. I officiated a year of high school games and then started working junior college ball. After a year of that, I started working DIII games. I officiated two years at that level, and then thought I was ready to work in the Big Ten. I drove to Chicago on my own dime, to talk to Bob Burson who was the Big Ten supervisor at the time, to tell him I was ready. I was confident. Bob was courteous to me.

He was a gentleman, polite and professional. He wasn't sure I was as ready as I thought I was. He said it was better to be sure you were ready then to get your chance too soon and mess it up. We talked for a half hour about me, my goals in officiating and I left for home. A couple of weeks later I was utterly shocked; he hired me to work on the Big Ten Independent Staff, which was no league games but games involving Notre Dame, Marquette, Dayton and DePaul.

I was thrilled, because it was a great start. My first game was at Notre Dame, something I have never forgotten.

I was excited. At one point, I put the ball in play on the baseline. I did everything you are supposed to do, but did not put the whistle in my mouth. I handed the ball to the in-bounder, who dropped it. And, it rolled in the lane. About eight players jumped on the ball in a scrum that was a mess. I couldn't get hold of my whistle. Finally, I got the whistle in my mouth, blew it, stopped a play that had never started. The in-bounder dropped the ball and I couldn't get the whistle in my mouth to stop the play and start over. Maybe Bob was right; I probably wasn't ready.

● ● ● ● ●

Of all the things you get asked when people know you officiate college basketball games, there are two recurring themes. "Which coaches are the best and worst to work with?" and "What do you say to the coaches when you are over there talking to them?"

Those are the things people seem to want to know. It is not appropriate to discuss the best/worst list, because no real good can come from that. However, I do have a list of things that I say to coaches and players.

There is no magic in those conversations, and many times it is a lot less heated and confrontational than you might think. Sometimes the coach just wants someone to talk to or vent to; other times it is just "how have you been, and how is the family" type stuff. But if they are really mad at me, or at one of my partners, these are my "go-to" phrases that often work in those moments of heated conversations:

"Coach, just talk to me man-to-man, what's wrong? What is bothering you?"

"Coach, your team needs you. You can win this game. But you can't win it if you are going to try and referee and coach. Agree?"

"You have to help me here. My supervisor is on my back about you staying in the box and acting right, and I do not want to have to do something that wouldn't be good for your kids, so can you help me?"

"That last call I made was awful. I am really sorry. I won't let that happen again."

"You are way too good of a coach to act like this."

"My partner will be over here in just a minute and he can explain that call then, okay?"

"You have to let it go. We are going to miss a play now and then, but you have to move on."

"Please, do what you do best, coach your guys."

"Your team cannot win if you are not engaged with them."

"I would never, ever, try to show you up or embarrass you. I would expect you to treat me the same way."

"You can yell at me about that play all you want but I was not the guy who blew the whistle."

"Please find another word to use beside that one." (when you hear an inappropriate word; and a few specific words come to mind.)

"Could you help me with your player number 15 (or whichever one is giving you a problem), he cannot react to every play."

"Coach, I will talk to you as much as is necessary, but I am not going to have your assistants trying to referee every play. If they continue to do that, it is going to cause a bad deal."

"You need to give my partner a chance."

"Coach, you need to give me a chance here."

"We are going to try and let you play, but this has gone too far.

You need to help us."

TO PLAYERS:

"Be legal, straight up, do not hold each other." (say that same thing at both ends of court.)

"Find another word."

"We will let you play, but you cannot play that physical."

"Your teammate number 15 (or whomever) is going to cost you a technical foul with me unless you straighten him out for me."

"You are the best player on the court, act like it."

"Why would you let that guy number three get to you, you are so much better than him. He couldn't guard you ever." Then you go to number 15, who was getting into it with number three and say the exact same thing to him.

"There is a responsibility that goes with being the best player on the court. You are the best player on the court. I need you to act like it and help me here."

Most of those statements are standard "Hartzell speak" when dealing with coach or player issues. An attitude of being "firm but friendly" usually works. And, if you draw a line in the sand in terms of how far coaches or players can go with you, then you cannot continue to move the line.

•••••

Curtis Shaw, my current supervisor in the Big 12, C-USA and AAC, was a one-of-a-kind referee — by the book, no leeway, all business, no BS. Most guys give and take a little on the court, but not Curtis. I had tremendous respect for him then and now.

He is a friend. He had a great career. He's fun to be around, had a background a lot like me, grew up poor without much stuff, made it through hard work.

He and I set a record one night in Orlando. During warm-ups, one of the young players for Vanderbilt violently dunked the ball. That is against the rules. Two-shot technical foul to start the game. A bad way to start, but it had to be done. Everyone saw it and you could not look away from it.

As we got ready to start the second half, we were waiting for TV to give us the thumbs up so we could put the ball in play. While we waited, one of the players awaiting the inbounds pass gave his opponent a forearm to the chest.

Curtis' whistle went off. Dead ball technical foul. Two shots. We started both halves with a technical foul. I said to Curtis after the game, "Well, we set a record tonight, started both halves with a technical foul."

•••••

I officiated a lot of Big Ten games with Ed Hightower, referenced earlier in this book. I loved working with Ed. There was no garbage in the game, ever. On this night they were working at Wisconsin with Tom O'Neill. It was a good crew, and I expected a good night. On the way to the game from Chicago, where we met to drive to Madison, Ed was his usual self, busy on the cell phone managing all the aspects of his real job as a superintendent of schools. He was good at it, and worked hard at it. He kept busy with it all the way up to pregame on most nights. On this night Ed was on the phone on the whole trip and all the way in the arena to the locker room.

Tommy O'Neill is a fun-loving guy — happy, always teasing and kidding, fun to be around. As the pregame time wore on, the crew was getting dressed and doing their pregame talk, which got interrupted on occasion by Ed's phone ringing with an after-hours emergency. They got close to the 30-minute mark when officials are supposed to be on the court to observe warm-ups by the teams, a rule every official hated. Ed's phone rang again. He managed the crisis and finished getting dressed.

Just as the three were to leave the locker room, Ed's phone rang again. This time, it was Tom, in a bathroom stall in our locker room, calling Ed.

"Who is this?" Ed said.

"Ed, it's me, Tom," said O'Neill.

I am dying of laughter.

"What do you mean it's you, Tom?," said Ed.

"Ed, I just wanted to know what time are we going on the court,?" O'Neill said to Hightower over the phone.

O'Neill, ever the jokester, pulled one over on the great Ed Hightower. I loved it. And, so did Ed.

•••••

Everyone thinks the coaches and referees have huge problems with each other. Not true. I have the utmost respect for these coaches who work so hard and do their best to develop young men and not only their basketball talents, but do their best to develop them as people and future citizens as well. I am a big fan of college athletics. It is not nearly as bad nor corrupt as people think. And 98 percent of the guys coaching on the men's side, where my experience lies, are terrific people, good guys, who treat people right and professionally.

I could list dozens of favorite guys, but I would leave someone out so I won't do that, but some that have the worst reputations as guys who are tough on the sidelines are some of the best, and I have real life examples. Bob Knight sent flowers when my mom died. Gene Keady called me after he retired and we talked to each other in a professional way and in a friendly and forgiving manner even though our on-the-court relationship was not the greatest.

Bill Self sent me a note in regard to his poor behavior one night. Rick Barnes always wants to talk about racing with me. Greg McDermott and Ben Jacobson are two of the finest people I have ever met. I never see Coach K when he does not ask about my kids. And on and on.

These coaches get a bad rap. They are educators and mentors, in addition to their coaching duties. One night three years ago at Alabama, I got hit head-on by two players and knocked into the scorer's table and broke two ribs. It was awful. I couldn't breathe and had to try and take a few days off before getting back on the court. Anthony Grant, the coach at Alabama at the time, called me three times to see if I was okay. That meant a lot to me, and that is what a lot of coaches would have done. I was always known as a "coaches AD" in the administration business and nothing that has happened to me on the refereeing side has changed my positive opinion of many great basketball coaches around the country.

•••••

When my little guy, Jackson came along and was old enough to know what I was doing when I left the house to referee games, he and I decided we would do something to bond us to each other and help us think about each other when we were apart. We decided that during basketball season we would both paint the toenails on our big toes bright red. So we did. We thought it was funny. But, I sure got some funny looks in the dressing rooms from my officiating partners when I took off my socks.

•••••

One of the things that I like about the officiating business is the give-and-take between coaches and officials. One night at Purdue, the veteran Michigan State coach, Jud Heathcote, said to me, "Hey Rick, are you related to the Big Dog (Glen Robinson) — you give him every stinking call." I turned to Coach Heathcote and said, "Jud, I am related to him just the same as I was to Steve Smith (former Michigan State star)." I thought it was a great off-the-cuff response. So did Jud. He and Tom Izzo (his assistant at the time) died laughing.

•••••

As referenced earlier in this book, I came from a small, north central Iowa farm town. I got a good education and graduated somewhere in the middle of a high school class of 36. I had a great ACT test score and could have gone several places to college, but chose UNI because my dad was sick and I wanted to be close to home, and the university wanted me to play football and baseball. I did not take a student deferment for the military draft because I knew it would break my dad's heart.

My draft lottery number was 129. The year before they had taken guys up to number 175. If you were drafted in those days, you were on the first plane to Viet Nam. Not a good thing.

My first two academic semesters yielded a stellar 2.08 and 2.06 grade point average (GPA). Not very good. I was on an athletic and academic scholarship, so after the second semester, I had to go see my advisor, whom I shall call here, Mr. Dennis. He was a good guy, he really helped me and I knew he believed in me and wanted me to succeed.

I walked into his office in the basement of Gilchrist Hall for our meeting. He looked at my grades. He looked at me. And, even though you could not do this now, you could do it then, I guess; he reached over the desk, grabbed me by the shirt and pulled my face about two inches from his. He said, "If you keep getting grades like this, you will either be back on that farm milking cows the rest of your miserable life or you will be on the way to see how good of a soldier you can be in Viet Nam. Now, get the hell out of my office." Ouch. He was right. I decided that I needed to get my act in gear.

My dad was sick and dying at the time or he would have said the very same thing to me. After that meeting, I went to work. My last six semesters at UNI I never had a GPA under 3.2. My M.A. GPA was 3.7. My Ph.D. grade point average was over 3.5. Mr. Dennis was right. I was capable of much better. Thank you, sir.

●●●●●

My dad was a World War II veteran. He served in the European Theatre and even though he did not talk about the war much, nor did his war buddies, I know it had a huge impact on him. He was an administrative assistant of some sort, but he never explained to me exactly what he did during the war. He did tell this story, over and over, about coming home from the war on a boat, across the Atlantic Ocean. He used to tell this story often, and he thought it was so hilarious. I heard it a lot, and I laughed every time he told it, because I knew I was supposed to do that. My dad was standing on the deck of the boat on the way home from the war, and friend of his, a black man from Georgia, was standing there with him and they were talking. My dad looked out over the ocean and said, "Man there sure is a lot of water out there." And, according to dad, his friend said, "Yep, and you are only seeing the top of it." And, that is the story. My dad thought it was one of the funniest things he had ever heard.

•••••

Basketball carries a differing amount of weight in different places. In the Southeast, football reigns supreme and except for a couple of schools, basketball is just an interlude between football season and spring football season. Steve Gordon (one of my dearest friends) and I worked an ACC league game at Florida State one night vs. Georgia Tech. Georgia Tech had a great player named Matt Harpring. The game went three overtimes, and stayed close all the way — a nail biter.

All the plays fell just right for us and we were really good in the game. Florida State won at the buzzer. There was no national television, the game was not in the spotlight. Steve calls it the "greatest game no one saw." That is exactly right. We got in the car after the game, still pumped from a great job and ready now to relax and drive back to Jacksonville where we were staying. Steve said, "Turn on the post-game and see what they have to say about the game." I did. The first question in the call-in show after the game was a caller from Pensacola. "Hey, what do you think of the quarterback the Seminoles got coming in next fall?" So much for a huge basketball game, nearly perfectly officiated and well played.

•••••

The "Pit" in Albuquerque is an iconic basketball venue. National championships have been played there and the rabid New Mexico Lobo fans go crazy every home game. The journey from the floor of the Pit to the locker rooms for the teams and officials is up a very steep and long tunnel. It is a pain to walk up and down when you have to go to and from the floor.

I worked there one night when New Mexico played Utah. Utah was coached at the time by one of the great men, coaches and characters in all of college basketball, Rick Majerus. Rick was a big man. Basketball was his life He was single, lived in a Marriott Hotel, and coached basketball. He was always great with the officials. On this night, his team trailed by 12 points at the half, at New Mexico. As halftime started we all headed toward the entrance to the tunnel. The three of us who were officiating started up the tunnel first, and as usual the teams ran past us on the way to their locker rooms. I glanced back over my shoulder to see Coach Majerus, by himself, struggling with the steep climb up the ramp. I stopped, went back to him and asked if he needed help, and if I could help him in any way.

He put his arm around my shoulders and his other hand on the guard rail and we went up the ramp together. All the way to the top. At the top he slapped me on the backside, said "thanks" and we all went our own way. It was a moment that I cannot ever forget. An official, with the visiting coach (down 12 points on the road) arm in arm, up the ramp at New Mexico. Rick and I always got along before that, and after that. Nothing was ever said about it by either of us. I have always thought the relationship between the referees and the coaches did not need to be dysfunctional or adversarial. Everyone do their job. Work hard. Do what you have to do. But, care about each other. It isn't that hard.

●●●●●

Sometimes in the officiating business you get booed. Fans go crazy. It has gotten worse over the years in terms of the names you get called and the things people say to you. The Tim Donaghy gambling situation brought out those comments, which never sit well with the officials. I have heard a lot of comments over the years, including:

"How do you get that size 38 ass in those size 34 pants?"

"Hey Hartzell, how is your wife...and my kids?"

"Hey ref, you have 'audubin hair'—ought to been on a dog's ass."

Of course, the old standards:

"Go back to Foot Locker."

"Three Blind Mice."

"Hey ref, you forgot your glasses."

"You are too _____, _____, _____, (fill in the blank with your favorite word here) old, fat, stupid, or all the above."

"Hey ref, you are absolutely killing us!" (My favorite, because I am never sure who 'us' is.)

I have been on crews that have been booed unmercifully. One night at Purdue, my friend Sid Rodeheffer made nine straight calls that went against the Boilermakers. He just would not let either one of us, his partners, take a call to ease his pain. The last one of the half was from about 70 feet, a travel, and it just did not have to be called. The fans went out of their minds and booed for five minutes straight, non-stop. We got to the locker room and before I could even say anything Sid said, "The hell with them. I am not stopping." I encouraged Sid to reconsider. And he did. But they kept booing the whole rest of the game. It was a long night.

•••••

In the ACC tournament, one year I had Duke vs. North Carolina. It was never as hard a game in the tournament as it was during the regular year, but it still was not easy. I had a call at the end of the first half where Steve Wojciechowski (Wojo) had the ball near the half court line. He pivoted away from the defender and when he did, the defender came right up on him, straddling his front leg. Wojo came forward, hit the defender in the chest and knocked him over. The defender was not in legal guarding position, he cannot straddle the leg and be in the offensive player's space. This play was a block and that is how I called it. It was a predominantly UNC crowd and they were sure I was wrong. We got booed off the court. But, the solace that I had was that I knew I was right, regardless of what the crowd thought

•••••

Mike Wood and I worked a lot of games together. We had several great games and excellent chemistry, and a long-time friendship which continues to this day. Mike was a superior play caller and a guy who could make the game work. He was terrific with coaches. We always seemed to get games at Georgia Tech that became controversial.

We had a shooter knocked over the bench with no call from one of our partners; we had a last second tip-in that Mike called no good in the days before replay; we had a game where our supervisor kicked the phone off a table in the locker room when it rang because he was so mad at us; and on and on it goes. But we did come up with a novel idea one night. We were booed when leaving the court at halftime at Tech. When we made our way

down the long tunnel to the court for the second half, we happened to get there the very same time as the home team, Georgia
Tech. As they were going on the court, Mike and I looked at each
other and just got in line with them and ran on the court at the
same time they did. The fans can't boo and cheer at the same
time. We snuck to our spots with nary a boo and made it through
the second half unscathed. Next time you go to a game, see if the
refs go on the court with the home team if they have had a tough
first half. Mike and I think we invented that little trick.

One Christmas break, Wood and I were called, at our homes,
and asked by our supervisor to get to El Paso, Texas, for their
Holiday Tournament. It seems that the University of Texas was
playing in the tournament and they required UTEP to have ACC
officials instead of the officials they had contracted. The UTEP
vs. UT rivalry is a heated one since UTEP has won the only national championship in basketball ever in the state of Texas and
they announce that every home game. So, the newspapers made
a big deal of Texas only playing if ACC guys worked the games.
Wood and I and some other ACC guys went to El Paso and they
booed us when we pulled in the parking lot — continuously for
three games each. No fun. But, it is also the time Mike and I
went to Juarez, Mexico, just to say we did it. We were about a
quarter mile into Juarez when we realized we were some place
we shouldn't be so we did a u-turn and left. The border guards
did not boo us.

•••••

I have worked games in just about all the great arenas in the
country. Pauley Pavilion, the Pit, the Marriott Center in Pro-
vo (very hard place to work), the Hoosier Dome, the Louisiana
Superdome, the MetroDome and the Carrier Dome. Cameron

Indoor, the old building at Maryland, the Dean Smith Center, Madison Square Garden and the Palestra, just to name a few. I have had the backboard torn down in warm-ups, the ceiling leak, the scoreboards not work or go out during the game, lights shut off, tornado alarms sound, and on and on. I was at the University of Illinois the night they honored and retired Chief Illiniwick. I was in the arena the night Lenny Wirtz threw out the Georgia Tech mascot, the bee. I have left Morgantown, West Virginia, having four grey-haired 80-year-old women calling me the worst names you could ever imagine. I worked at UNLV when they had the great teams and they had fans in what they called "Gucci Row" where you felt really uncomfortable about what they expected from you in regard to the outcome. You get enough games and you just about see it all.

I worked at Tallahassee one night when Florida State played North Carolina. I believe it was Coach Smith's last season at UNC. When we got to Tallahassee, the temperature was an unusually cold 50 degrees. We got to the arena and it was under construction, which we knew about and everyone was ready for. However, they had taken all of the tarpaulin coverings off the open windows and the arena was below 50 degrees during pregame. It was cold, too cold to play or at least play effectively. I was the referee on the game so I called the ACC office and my supervisor, Fred Barakat, to find out what he wanted us to do. He was in a tough spot and told me to use my best judgment. So, I went to the UNC locker room to see Coach Smith, expecting some push-back to playing the game. We talked and he finally said, "Well, it is the same for them and we want to go home so we will play." I thought that was great.

I suggested we give the teams an extended warm-up and that we would start the game 45 minutes late. Coach Smith agreed.

I talked to Leonard Hamilton, the FSU coach, and he agreed. All is well. I called the ACC office and Fred agreed, nice job. I went to our officials' locker room and the UNC star player, Vince Carter, was sitting there in our locker room and talked to us for about half an hour. I finally said, "Hey Vince, don't you think you should go to your warm-up." His eyes twinkled and he said, "I don't think I will have any problem being in the starting lineup tonight." He was right. We played. No sweating on this night. But, I will always remember Coach Smith being so accommodating on a night when he didn't have to be, for sure.

•••••

Dave Odom, coach at Wake Forest, was always a little tough for me to deal with. I don't think he bought my act. I had nothing against him, and he had some great teams. One particular year he had the great Tim Duncan and a guard named Randolph Childress. They were awesome together, and won the ACC tournament.

In their regular season game at Florida State, we had a crazy play happen and it caused all hell to break loose. Duncan went to the basket to score and got fouled. The ball flew out of his hands, he re-caught it and shot, and it went in the bucket. I called the foul on the first contact, before he re-caught the ball, and was going to give him two shots. The call was 100 percent correct.

Either Coach Odom did not see what happened, did not know the rule or just wanted to be cantankerous; he went out of his mind. I could not talk to him. He stomped and yelled and carried on. Technical foul. He still would not stop. More of the same. Technical foul again, this one on an assistant coach, so I did not have to throw Coach Odom out of the game. You have to leave the gym on your second technical foul, so I gave this one to his assistant, Ricky Stokes. He knew what I was doing.

So, we go to the Florida State end and shoot four free throws. Then we come back to the Wake Forest end and shoot Duncan's two free throws. Everything done right, the right call, the right T's, the right procedure. After the game, my supervisor came in the locker room. He looked at me and said, "I know what you called. You were right. But sometimes it is smarter to be wrong than to be right." What? He was saying that the avenue of least resistance would have been to count the basket on Tim Duncan's re-catch and shot. His logic — no one would have known the difference. No controversy, and no technical fouls needed, no angst from Coach Odom. I knew better than to argue or say anything, but it was not in my DNA to do it that way, regardless of who the coach was.

There is an interesting sidelight to this true story. My supervisor at the time, the aforementioned Fred Barakat, was often very hard on me. He wanted me to be good, he saw something in me, I know that. But, at times, he was very, very hard on me. Unfair, I often thought. After this particular game he called me and asked for my careful description about what exactly happened on the play with Tim Duncan that led to the subsequent issue with Coach Odom and the technical foul. I described it in detail just as I have here.

He was silent on the other end of the phone for what seemed like forever. I knew what was coming next was not going to be good for me to hear. He said, "Sometimes it is better to be wrong, than it is to be right." And, he hung up the phone. That was it. Nothing more was ever said about what happened that night at Florida State. I thought long and hard about what he really meant by that statement. He meant that if I was the only one who really knew what happened on the play, and if I could have taken the "avenue of least resistance" then I should have done that. Or at least I think that is what he meant. You

*can see why the officiating business gets confusing sometimes for the
people who are out there doing the work.*

• • • • •

In my dual life as a Division I Director of Athletics and a Division I referee, some odd things occurred. There were very few conflicts and almost all the relationships I had with other administrators were positive. I believe almost everyone accepted what I did, that I did it reasonably well and was fair.

Most coaches and other AD's knew that I understood how important the games were and that I tried as hard as I could every night to do the best job. However, one night at Illinois, they were playing Arkansas-Little Rock (UALR) and something unusual happened.

The AD at UALR was a guy named Chris Petersen. He grew up in Macomb, Illinois, where his dad was the AD at Western Illinois and was a dear friend of my mentor, Stan Sheriff, the AD at Northern Iowa. Chris was always good to me.

I worked a lot of UALR games in the Sun Belt. This night they were on the road in Champaign, IL. I made a call that went against UALR, and as I reported the foul, I saw this guy at the table, at the UALR radio spot, make a motion in my direction, throwing his hands down toward me, in regard to the call. I didn't think much of it, maybe it was not intended for me, it just didn't bother me.

A bit later in the game after another call that went against UALR, I saw the same guy give me the "choke" sign. When I looked closer, I found it to be Chris, who was doing the color for the UALR radio broadcast. I looked again, got closer and said, "Was that intended for me?" He gave me the choke sign again.

I threw him out. Made him leave the table and the arena. No technical foul, I didn't want to penalize the team. But, I could not put up with that. I did it quickly, no fanfare. As luck would have it, the following March (this game was in December), UALR hosted the NCAA first and second round games at their downtown arena in Little Rock. I was assigned there, and Chris Petersen was the host administrator. He met us for our pre-tournament meeting, hosted the breakfast we had, and met us at our locker room before the games. He could not have been nicer. It was just like old times, cordial, cracking jokes, fun. He never said a word about what happened at Illinois that night and neither did I. It was like it never happened. Ted Hillary was with me both when I threw Chris out and at the NCAA tournament in Little Rock. He and I have laughed about this situation dozens of times.

•••••

In my fifth year at UNI as the AD, in about 2004, we were playing Creighton in our newly-opened McLeod Center. We had worked very hard to turn an awful basketball program into a great one. I hired Greg McDermott and he worked miracles. We went from 6-25 and 150 season tickets the year before I hired him to the NCAA tournament, a new building and 3,000 season tickets. He did the finest job of building a program that any coach could possibly do. He and I worked hand-in-hand to do it; he did the heavy lifting and I supported him. It was a lot of fun.

But, we never could beat Creighton. On this night we had a chance. I was sitting courtside watching the game that had three of my good friends officiating — Ed Hightower, Gerry Pollard and J.D. Collins. Late in the game, UNI was pressuring Creighton near half court. The game was tied. UNI needed a stop and a basket to win. It was a huge crowd, and a big game for the Panthers. The Creighton point guard got trapped near the half line and when he dribbled, he inadvertently dribbled the ball in back court. It should have been a back court violation, and a turnover, but no whistle came. The crew did not see the play.

Ed Hightower was the closest official. I could not believe he missed the play. I jumped up and quite honestly, acted stupid. I wanted that call for our team, our coach, our fans. I reacted. And, I was wrong to do it. Ed and I were (are) friends. What I did was wrong and everybody saw me do it. I have apologized to Ed, J.D. and Gerry a hundred times each by now. It was out of character for me. I took on the role of fan for a second and it was a huge mistake that I am embarrassed by to this day. Thankfully, they all understood and they respected me and my position and rooting interest enough to forgive me. Stupid behavior by yours truly.

•••••

One of the things that makes me the most proud is that almost no one ever accused me of a conflict of interest while working games and serving as an AD. I never worked in the Patriot League (when I was AD at Bucknell) or Missouri Valley (while at UNI) at that time and never had a game that directly impacted either school where I was the AD.

I suppose you could have gone on a tangential path and make some connection to some game, but I never, ever thought about Bucknell or UNI and how any game I officiated would possibly be good or bad for them if the result went a particular way. At Wisconsin one night late in the season in 2006, they were playing Indiana, and Indiana was on the NCAA tournament bubble at the time. Wisconsin beat them when I put the Badgers on the line late in the game on an Indiana foul. The Indiana people never said a word. My supervisor (Rich Falk) said the call was 100 percent correct. The TV announcers never blinked. But, Doug Gottleib, on his national radio show and on ESPN, made a big deal out of the fact that Indiana was on the bubble, as was UNI, and the call that I made hurt Indiana, subsequently, according to his logic, helping UNI. He would not let it go, would not stop his criticism of me. He had people calling my President (of UNI). They contacted me for a comment. No one responded, and it went away. And, I got a lot of support from all over the college basketball world about the matter, including from some name coaches, administrators and others. The situation died down. Gottleib never tried to talk to me about it.

It was similar to a situation with the announcer Billy Packer, who went after me for a call, something I cannot forget. Both cases were unfair. The announcers were uninformed. They never asked me about my view, opinion or decision-making. Almost all of the TV and radio guys you meet are fair and understanding of how hard the refereeing job is, and you always greet them and try to help them with their work when you are officiating. Not so, from me, for Mr. Gottleib. Sorry, cannot do it. He was unfair, cruel and personal. And, that wasn't right.

•••••

My kids have traveled with me often in my officiating career. There are a million stories. One night in a snowstorm at the Meadowlands I worked the Villanova-Rutgers game. The snow storm made the game late. When I came out for pregame warm-ups, my son Nate, about 12 at the time, was in the layup line with the Villanova team. There were about 20 people in the whole arena and they asked him to join them.

My daughter, Amanda, went up to a lady at Penn State who

was yelling one night at me, and giving me a bad time. Amanda was about eight. I saw her do it, and after the game I asked what she said. Amanda said she told the woman, "That referee you are screaming at is my dad. I love him. Please leave him alone." I was proud of her for doing that. And, I bet the lady stopped yelling.

Nate and I were driving home from Syracuse one night in February, in a blizzard. The weather was awful but I had work to finish and had to get Nate back to school for the next day. We got run off the road by a truck driver who didn't see us, and we were up on the guard rail in my Pontiac. No one was hurt, we were just on top of the snow and guardrail, and stuck. We did everything we could to get out, but to no avail. Finally, a semi-truck stopped and asked if we needed help, or a ride. We explained our dilemma. The driver came over, pushed and lifted and grunted, and got our car off that guard rail by himself, back on the road. He probably moved the car six feet by himself. We got in and drove off. The darnedest thing I have ever seen. Home safe a couple of hours later. Unbelievable.

●●●●●

No compilation of referee stories would be complete without some "driving in the middle of the night" stories. I have a bunch of them because I drove a lot to get back to work after games. It was the only way to stay on top of my full-time job. Typically, I would leave work as late as possible, drive or fly (mostly drive), get to the game, work it, and get in the car and go back home. There were a lot of opportunities for driving issues, problems or complications.

If you talk to anyone who officiates sports, they will tell you about driving late at night, with a soda in the cup holder, a sandwich between your legs, and driving in bad weather when the cell phone rings from someone who cares about you is on the line. There are stories about trucks cutting you off, snowstorms, rainstorms, or being late and getting arrested. There are a million of these stories. Everybody has them.

•••••

I landed at the Hartsfield-Jackson International Airport one Friday night in late January, for a game at Georgia Tech the next day. I had heard the weather was not good in Atlanta, but we landed without an issue. I got off the plane and walked through a deserted airport. We were the last flight that landed — they closed the airport given the bad weather. It was icy, with a little snow. In the Midwest, we wouldn't even have blinked in regard to this weather, but in Atlanta it was like Armageddon. Everything was closed. No buses were running, no taxi's. I had a reservation at the Airport Marriott, probably three miles from the terminal. I walked, pulling my carry-on bag and my briefcase. It was slippery, cold, and a mess. But, there was no other way to get there. I made it at about 2:00 a.m. The people at the Marriott desk looked at me like I was a homeless person trying to find a spot to land. As a referee, out there traveling, it feels just like that a lot of nights.

•••••

In basketball terms, you must stay focused, engaged and keep your concentration until the final whistle. A team can come from 15 points behind in the last five minutes to win. The refereeing landscape is littered with stories of officials who worked the perfect game for 39 minutes and 48 seconds only to mess up the game so badly in the last 12 seconds that it could not be fixed. I have "been there and done that," and anyone who officiates major college or professional sports, or a good high school schedule has been there too; if they say they haven't, then they are not telling the truth. Every minute of every game is important to someone. People do not forget that you messed up the game, even though you were near-perfect for the first 39:48.

•••••

I was a high school quarterback. I went to UNI thinking maybe I could be good enough to be the backup guy there. And, I think I could have been, but they recruited over me, and rightfully so. I could throw it, but I couldn't run well enough. They tried me at tight end, long snapper, holder for field goals and all of that. I was just about good enough. I was a JV football legend for two years. Started a few games and did okay. Won a few, threw some TD passes. One day in my sophomore year, we played a JV game at Luther College. None of the other QB's played well, and we were getting beat 21-0 at the start of the fourth quarter when they put me in the game. I threw for a touchdown and ran for two more and we lost 21-20. I pitched it all over the lot for a quarter. I was Joe Namath for 15 minutes. The coaches told me after that game I was going to get a chance after that performance to play more. Not true, didn't happen. I am not mad about it, I just wasn't good enough; I knew that then and I know that now. But, that day, I had my moment in the sun. It was a tremendous thrill to lead a team back to a near victory in a physical game where you got knocked down and had to get up and where you had to be a leader and try to carry a team. There is nothing like football, even for all the negatives of injuries and concussions and bumps and bruises. There is no other thrill like that, to me.

•••••

I have been involved in thousands of games as a player, coach, administrator and official. In almost none of those in which I played, coached or served as an administrator do I remember anything that any of the officials did that impacted the game.

Oh sure, there were games when there were some bad calls, but as an athletic director I always thought that if my team played well enough then the officiating would not really matter, no matter how poor it might have been on that given night. Instead, what I remember are other things from games that were more personal in nature.

A few of my memories:

(1) I was head high school football coach at Tri-County High School in Iowa. We were not very talented, but I had good kids who played hard and gave their all each day. We played a long-standing Iowa power one night, WACO High School. This night, they were beating us 54-7 late in the fourth quarter. Their coach, an Iowa High School Hall of Fame coach, called timeout three times in the last two minutes so they could score again to beat us 61-7. I was steaming. He had embarrassed my team, and me personally. At the post-game handshake, I told him so. I will never forget that. And, it is hard to forgive.

(2) While the AD at Bucknell, we tried hard to build a winning football program. It was difficult for many reasons. I finally got my part right with the facilities and scheduling, and I hired a great new coach, Tom Gadd — a good man. He performed a miracle. In his first team meeting, when I introduced him

to the team, I knew we had it right, we were going to build a winner. Tom stood off to the side of the room as I introduced him. I will never forget what happened next.

He looked at about 75 kids sitting in that room. The room were absolutely silent for what seemed like 10 minutes; it was probably 45 seconds total. He looked them over and then with the most confidence I have ever heard from a coach of a program that had not had a winning season in over 35 years, said the following: "Okay, I am not going to talk long, but I want you to listen and listen carefully. First thing is this. Turn your hats around on your heads or take them off. Sit up straight, get your feet off the chairs. Put your eyes right up here on mine. Tomorrow, we are going to work. We are going to work harder than any of you have ever worked, guaranteed. We will be the most well-conditioned team in this league when the season starts next fall. We will be the strongest team from our work in the weight room, and we will play the right way. You will do your studying and take care of your grades and be on track to graduate on time or you will not play. You will behave out in the community, or you won't play. You will do some community service, or you won't play.

And, for any who think I am not serious, then the back door to this room is wide open and you are free to leave right now. We are going to win a championship here. And, we are going to do it with anybody in this room who decides to stay and work. If you don't want to do that, leave now with no questions asked, no hard feelings. We will practice at 4 p.m. tomorrow. See you then." And the meeting was over. Less than two years from that day, Bucknell beat Colgate in Lewisburg when a young man named Brandon Little knocked down a pass in the end zone to secure the Bison win, and the Patriot League championship. Unbelievable. No one, including me, thought it was possible. Tom Gadd, a tremendous coach and man, did.

(3) I have played in a lot of football, basketball, baseball, softball games in my time — national tournaments, national amateur championship games, softball world championship games, and so on. My most vivid athletic memory, however, is an odd one. I played quarterback for the freshman football team at UNI. I could throw it some, but mobility and quickness were not my strengths. We played some junior college teams and some local Division III teams. One night in Cedar Falls, against Ellsworth JC, a perennial power, I was playing quarterback and having a decent night, threw for a couple of touchdowns. In the middle of the third quarter, I threw an interception. I was mad at myself and started toward the sideline to try and get in the way of the defender who intercepted the pass. I can still remember the flash in front of me. One of the interceptor's fellow defenders hit me so hard from the side that I ended up out-of-bounds on my face, knocked out. He drilled me in the ear-hole and I had slobber coming out of my mouth. I can still feel the sensation. Of all the memories to have indelibly etched in your brain!

(4) I have thrown out one head coach in my 35 year officiating career. I will never forget the circumstances that led up to it. The game was George Washington (GW) at St. Bonaventure in Olean, New York, where St. Bonaventure is located, a tough place to get to in the winter. Usually the visiting team and officials are grumpy, and the home team has a huge advantage. On this night, I was with two great professional referees, John Koskinen (Kos) and John Bonder, both of Philadelphia. We were working the game and Kos, the old pro of the bunch, hit GW coach John Kuester with a technical foul. No big deal,

just a part of the game. Then, a few minutes later, still in the first half, John Bonder did the same. This was in the days when you got three technical fouls as a coach before you had to leave the gym. Sure enough, at the start of the second half, Kuester decided it was my turn in the box. He would not stop. He was on my back, and said, "You don't have the guts to throw me out!" He was wrong. Technical foul. Three of them. See ya, Coach Kuester. The only throw-out of my career, and I am not really proud of it. For some reason, this incident bothers me to this day. I am not sure what was going on. I think Coach Kuester either wanted to go or to see if I would do it, if I had the courage. But, just maybe, an older and more mature Rick Hartzell could have kept him in the game.

•••••

One of my favorite "next generation" officials who is up-and-coming is Doug Sirmons.

Doug is really, really good, takes no garbage, is quick with his decisions, knows the rules and is a solid guy, too. We were assigned together at Vanderbilt one night, one of my favorite places to work. During the warm-up, I noticed the band, the Oak Ridge Boys (ORB), standing near the baseline. A lot of country music stars come to the Vandy games, so I did not think much of it. But then the Public Address announcer said that the ORB will be singing the national anthem. How cool! I told Doug the band was great, but he not only was not excited, he did not know who the Oak Ridge Boys even were.

When the anthem is played, the officials make a decision to stay on the court or go to the locker room, depending on how much time is left on the countdown clock.

I am a fast dresser and undresser and can get prepared for the tip-off in just a couple minutes after the warm-ups are over. Apparently, Doug needs a bit more time. He was the 'R' (referee) this night and he said, "We are going to the locker room." I complied, begrudgingly, and missed the national anthem sung by the Oak Ridge Boys. I tell Doug now that people say it was the greatest national anthem ever sung before a sporting event. And we missed it.

•••••

I easily remember the hardest calls I had in officiating. Like most officials, I have many memories to choose from, but two come immediately to my mind.

In one, my two pals, Frank Scagliotta (Scags) and Steve Gordon teamed with me on the Oklahoma-Texas game one year, in Austin. It's a tough game, though not quite at the level of the football rivalry. Kelvin Sampson was coaching Oklahoma and an old fast pitch softball rival of mine, and Tom Penders was coaching Texas. The game was close the entire way. On the last possession of regulation, l was at the trail position as Oklahoma inbounded the ball on a semi-fast break.

They had a player named Ryan Minor, who was a very good basketball player and a great athlete. He later played major league baseball for the Orioles. He caught the ball and turned up court and a Texas defender slid in front of him and there was a huge wreck. You would always like to pass on a play like that in that situation, so you don't have to decide the game, but the contact was violent and I had to call the play — a block on the Texas defender. One-and-one free throws for Minor, with the game tied. He makes the first, misses the second, Oklahoma wins. Tom Penders, a really decent guy, never forgave me. He still hasn't forgiven me. He never will forgive me. But I was right.

In the second instance, 1 worked the NCAA tournament in Phoenix in 2000, Florida vs. Gonzaga. Billy Donovan was the coach at Florida and Dan Munson at Gonzaga. Observers called it a great, close game, competitive and well played.

Gonzaga missed a shot with about 15 seconds left, and Florida's big man rebounded the ball. He got ready to throw the outlet pass and his teammate looked the other way. He traveled. I let it go. The drag of the pivot foot was minor, and I could live with not calling it. But then, he reestablished his balance and traveled again, 90 feet from the basket in a two-point game. Two travels. I had to call the second one, and take the ball away, and any chance for Florida to win — a tough situation. Billy Donovan, of whom I have the utmost respect, immediately asked me, "Rick, that call ends the game. Did you have to call it?" I explained that I did, I was sorry, but I had no choice. Gonzaga won the game. In the post-game press conference, Billy was asked about the call. He said, "Excellent official, a call that he had to make. No doubt about it, a travel." And, that was it. No controversy, no issues, no further scrutiny. Billy Donovan is a class act. He could have buried me, but he did not. I hold Billy in the highest regard.

●●●●●

One season in the late 1990s, Scags, Gordon and I worked the second North Carolina-Duke game in Durham. That game is considered a classic, regardless of the year. Afterwards, the three of us all checked into our hotel at the ACC tournament in Greensboro. There was a package for Steve and me, none for Scags.

I told Steve that we needed to look at the package right then. Sure enough, it was a tape from the game, sent by Dean Smith and his staff to Steve and to me, with the plays marked that they thought we missed. I don't have a problem with that process, but where was Frank's tape and his plays? He was great as usual; but he wasn't perfect. I looked at Steve. I thought for a minute. And, I gave the tape and the comments back to the desk clerk at the hotel and told them to tell the North Carolina staff that I did not accept the package. Steve did the same. I always had, and still have the greatest respect for Dean Smith. Nothing could ever change that, but I would not accept this tape or whatever plays they thought we missed. If they had sent a tape to all three of us, different story.

During the tournament, Coach Smith, who never missed a trick, said to me, "I hear you did not look at the tape I left for you at the hotel." I said, "No coach, I did not look at it." He looked at me and winked. He knew. I knew. It was all good. I think he respected the fact that I made a statement about what was right when I wouldn't look at it.

Oddly enough, Dean Smith's son, Scott, is a college basketball referee. We have become friends and talked a lot about his dad. Scott is a good man and was there for his dad right until the end. A nice story. Scott told me many times that his dad really respected me. And, that means a great deal to me.

·····

I have many Bobby Knight stories. Some can even be printed here. Some however, cannot.

I always got along with Knight, mainly because I understood his act. He was like the bully on the street corner who would steal your lunch on the way to school. If you let him do it he would keep right on stealing it. If you stopped it, you found that there was a real teddy bear inside that person. And he would respect you for taking care of business.

In his first year at Texas Tech, I had Knight's first round game at the Big 12 tournament in Kansas City.

His team was bad. He wanted the season to be over. He was extraordinarily grumpy. The game moved along, and Tech was getting beat. The game wasn't close. Like many coaches under those circumstances, Knight just wanted the game to be over so he could leave and get on with the other things in his life. He would try again next year with a new Red Raider team. The game was ragged — a lot of fouls, turnovers, the game dragging on. Knight yelled at me and said, "Don't call any more fouls or travels, I won't say a word. Let me get the hell out of here." While I agreed, we really couldn't do that; we had to call the plays that took place, with a little leeway for getting the game over.

With about five minutes left in the game, there was a huge commotion across the court from the team benches on press row. The crew and I had no choice but to temporarily stop the game.

Knight flew off the hook. "What the _____ is going on, let's play, the hell with all that crap over there," on and on. As the 'R' in the game, I went over to see what happened to cause the disruption. It became obvious that one of the members of the press corps covering the game had some sort of medical issue. I stood by, not trying to interrupt, but it was obvious we had to wait a few minutes to resume play; there were medical staff there, along with medical equipment on the court. I went to both coaches to explain. Knight was enraged. I finally told him that the man who was having an issue was his old friend from the Indianapolis paper, who was in Kansas City specifically to follow and report on Bobby's games in the tournament. Immediately, Knight changed.

I knew his friend was having a heart attack and told him that.

Knight looked at me and in the gentlest voice I have ever heard from him he said, "Will you walk over there with me?" I agreed and we walked across the court together where the man was lying after his medical issue. I waited there with Bobby until it was determined that his friend was going to be taken to the hospital and we could resume the conclusion of the game. I then walked Knight back to his bench. When we got there he looked me in the eye and said, "I am a real asshole sometimes, aren't I?" It was not the time for me to agree or disagree. I just put my hand on his shoulder, got him to sit down and told him we would get this game over as soon as possible so he could get to the hospital. He just said, "Thanks." And that is what we did. The man changed from a lion into a puppy dog in a matter of seconds. Hard not to like him, from my perspective.

My dear friend, John Higgins, of Omaha, is a terrific official and person. We have been friends a long time. John had to give Coach Knight a few technical fouls over his time working Texas Tech games. John would not be bullied and he and Coach Knight did not get along. It is usually the joke in officiating that if you do not want to go back to a place, then give a few technical fouls and you can avoid it. Lubbock, was one of those places.

Lubbock is considered a nice town, but it is hard to get to and get out of. If you have a 1 p.m. game or later on a Saturday, you are not getting out until Sunday. Officials hate that. And the winter weather there can suddenly get ugly. Lubbock comes in near the bottom of places to go to officiate.

Knight did not like John. The feeling was mutual. They decided just not to acknowledge each other or talk to each other to try and make the adversarial relationship work. One night at Tech with Higgins, he did not go to shake Coach Knight's hand by mutual agreement and with the support of the Big 12 office. I went to shake Knight's hand as usual. I had worked 50 of his games by this time in my career. We always got along. He would yell and curse and carry on, and he would let me do the same to him when I needed to or when he was wrong. On this night when I shook his hand he said to me, "I know you and Higgins are big friends. Your friend is an asshole." I looked right at him. Locked in with his eyes. "Well, you are wrong. He is not anything at all like you think he is. He just got tired of your crap and he dealt with it. He did what he had to do. He is a good man, a great dad and husband, a great official and you are wrong." And, that was it. He didn't ever bring it up again. I am not sure it changed his mind about John, but at least he knew where I stood on it. And, I think he respected me enough to realize that I might be right and he might be wrong. But, he would never admit that.

●●●●●

In the late 1990s, Georgia Tech had a string of great players who came through that program. The Barry brothers, Dennis Scott, Travis Best, Kenny Anderson, and one of my favorites, Matt Harpring. In his senior year, Harpring carried the team. Bobby Cremins coached Tech, and was considered every official's friend.

The guys loved Bobby. He never complained about the officiating, even when he should have. I worked Harpring's last game of his career, in the ACC tournament. With about three minutes left in his last game he fouled out. He was a crowd favorite in the ACC. Every fan respected his play and effort. When he fouled out, I had the ball in my hands for the free throws that were to be shot. I held the ball for at least two minutes while Harpring left the game to a standing ovation. I waited forever to put the ball in play. My pal Steve Gordon was working with me and he knew exactly what I was doing. A couple of trips later, I was at the Georgia Tech bench. Bobby Cremins looked at me and said, "Thanks for what you did for Matt." I had no idea he knew. It was a cool moment.

•••••

One night in 1990, Duke Edsall and I were working a game in Las Vegas. The ACC assigned most of the UNLV non-league games back then because "Tark" (UNLV Coach Jerry Tarkanian) wanted ACC officials for some reason. On this night, Duke and I were sitting at the bar at Caesar's Palace having a salad and an adult beverage. It was the night that Mike Tyson was fighting Buster Douglas for the heavyweight championship. The odds on the fight were like 50-1 in favor of Tyson. He had not been beaten at that point in his career.

I remember saying to Duke, "Man, I wish we could place a bet on this fight."

As officials we could not do that, and we knew it, but it was sure tempting to put $20 on Douglas at those odds. We laughed, because Douglas had no chance to win. Everyone knew that. About an hour later, after Buster knocked Tyson out, we both looked at each other knowing we could have made a lot more than our game check if we could have bet the fight and picked Douglas. But we followed the NCAA rules; no betting. Conscience clear. Billfold light.

•••••

As I have mentioned several times in this book, I worked a large number of Horizon League games in the late 1990s and early 2000s. I enjoyed the league, and John Adams, the supervisor at the time, gave me a lot of big games in the league.

I always seemed to get the Illinois-Chicago vs. UW-Milwaukee game at least once a year. There was a conflict between the coaches, Jimmy Collins of UIC and Bruce Pearl of UWM. That problem went back a lot of years from their times at Illinois and Iowa, respectively. Very simply, they did not like each other. They would not shake hands. There was a policeman at both benches. There was a lot of tension in the games. And, both teams were extremely good in the league, so the games were ultra-competitive.

One night in Chicago, I worked the game. One of my partners happened to be from Chicago and even though he was a great official, Coach Pearl was not buying his act.

Bruce was on my partner from the start of the game, and just would not let it go. He was mad on every play that went against his team. He stomped up and down the sideline, cursed, yelled and just acted inappropriately. Finally, he just went goofy. My partner called a technical foul on him and it was totally justified. It was early in the game, less than 10 minutes gone in.

I went over to Bruce and settled him down. We had known each other for a long time and there was mutual respect between us. Pearl apologized and cooled down, and I thought everything was under control.

We shot the technical foul and got ready to put the ball back in play. All of a sudden, Bruce walked down to the end of his bench and took both hands, and cleared off two large Gatorade coolers, about 50 full cups and some towels and other supplies. He threw everything off the table. I had no choice, obviously, and called a second technical foul. Bruce had to go to the locker room. I got to him, and to his credit, he knew, he had to go. I walked with him and on our way past my fellow official, who Bruce had the problem with and who called the first technical foul, Bruce took another verbal shot at him. So, I called another technical foul as he left the court to go to the locker room. Finally, we got him out of the arena. We shot the four additional technical foul shots and resumed the game.

I cannot recall for certain, but I believe UW-Milwaukee came back and won the game, with their head coach in the locker room. After the game, on my way back to Iowa, I called John Adams. I will never forget what he said. "I knew we had a problem when the head coach of the visiting team called me on his cell phone at 7:25 p.m. The game started at 7:05." He was right, we had a problem. But we did what we had to do. And Bruce and I have laughed about it a lot of times. He is a good guy, who just lost it on this night.

●●●●●

It is always a bad practice to start listing names of guys that you worked with over your basketball career who you really liked and cared about. It is inevitable you will leave someone out. But, these guys are so important because you work hard games with them and you go down the road with them. Nonetheless, I am going to do it. This is my book, my bucket list moment. Please indulge me. Here are some of my good guys, and a line about why:

"Tim Gattis: Tough. Been through a lot. A great man. An inspiration to me. And dear friend."

"Mike Wood: Long time pal. Big confidence, and the best play caller of our generation."

"Jim Burr: Tough. 15 Final Fours. Always showed me respect. In a Big East game, put me with him."

"Steve Welmer: Worked 120 games a year. Never saw a post foul he liked. Huge personality."

"Ted Hillary: 'The Tin Man.' A great official. Funny. Genuine."

"Tim Higgins: The best official of my generation, hands down. Knew exactly when the game needed a whistle. A great communicator. Give me him and Burr in any game, anywhere."

"John Higgins: A good man. A great official. Always looks great. And, got the success he deserved.'

"Curtis Shaw: Tough. By the book. No BS with him. The second fastest post-game dresser ever. A lion on the outside but soft as butter in his heart."

"Artie McDonald: Hard to describe. A true character. His appearance at my house once made my wife Kathy use the 'F' word for the only time I ever heard her curse. There is no one like Artie."

"Karl Hess: My long-time friend. A character. One-time wild man. Tough as nails. A Final Four fixture."

"Ed Hightower: A pro. Best manager of kids and coaches ever. All you had to do was call the plays if you were with Ed. He had the rest of it covered."

"Tom O'Neill: Funny. Happy. Gets the best dressed award. Everybody loves Tommy."

"Steve Olson: My Midwest pal. A country boy at heart. Excellent referee. Good man. He helped me so many times when I needed help."

"Tom Eades: Always steady and ready. Great fun to be with. Serious at game time and a riot after."

"Mark Whitehead: Terrific official. Always cared about me, my family. Never had a bad game with him. Loved to see his name on the line with mine in any game."

"Fred Barakat: My ACC supervisor. Gave me a chance. Chewed

me out. Made me better as a person and as an official. I miss him."

"Rich Falk: I worked for him at Northwestern as an assistant AD. I worked for him as an official in the Big 10. A pro all the way. The epitome of professionalism. One of the best people I have ever met."

"Jim Burch: 'Daddy Burch,' the last guy I worked a two-man game with and my Southern Conference supervisor. None better. The youngest looking man of his age, ever."

"Bobby Dibler: The best supervisor ever. He was an ex-official and he got it, he knew how to do his job. And, he let you do yours."

"Antinio Petty: 'Train' you are my pal. I love you man. One of the best guys ever.

"John Adams: Gave me the championship game in the Horizon League 9 straight times. Gotta like that guy. I was good for him and he was good to me."

"J.D. Collins: We were great friends and partners for a lot of years. I think I helped him as he lost his dad. We let it get away from us, for a petty reason, on my part. A very good man, bright. He is now the National Coordinator of Basketball officials, and he will do a great job."

"Joel Paige: My first partner, a lifelong friend who never had a bad day. Upbeat and gave me energy."

"Pat Brown: Another early partner, and a great football official too. He cared about me and checked in with me. Never got the big break, but never complained. First class."

"Hank Nichols: One of the all-time best officials ever. Great national coordinator. Put me in a lot of really big games when he didn't have to. I am indebted."

"Harold 'Pinky' Primrose: The mayor of Cedar Rapids, Iowa, he gave me my officiating start and mentored me as a baseball coach in my early years at Coe College. A wonderful man."

"Trent (TLove) Lovewell: He never met a stranger. Full of life and some other stuff as well. Turned out to be a great dad and husband. Amazing. Simply amazing."

"Gerald Beaudreaux: My partner, my supervisor (SEC) and my friend. Always sent me the nicest Christmas card. A true Cajun. Good man."

"Scott Thornley: One of the five best officials I ever worked with. Composed, professional, solid as a rock, the coolest smile in the world, retired too early. We needed him."

"Bruce Benedict: The old Braves catcher. I am a Braves fan for life. Could never get enough of Bruce's stories. Fun guy. Happy, and good to be with. We met late, but I call him a friend."

"Eric Curry: He let me mentor him. He let me advise him. I helped him, I think, and he helped me in a huge way. A good man, solid. I am proud of you, E."

Sam Lickliter: In a business littered with good guys, Sam was always one of the best. First class, always happy. An underrated official. But not underrated as a person to me.

"Kip Kissinger: Along with Doug Sirmons, James Breeding and Brett Hampton, one of best of the next generation. Gets better and better, and cares about other guys. Nice."

"Ron Groover: We always seemed to connect. A good family man who loves his kids. A great young official. I see me in him."

"Davey Hall: I never had a bad game with Dave. He cares a lot about his work. Out of a different mold, but I always liked and respected him."

"Randy McCall: I gravitated to him because I thought we were a lot alike. A really good man, excellent official, a leader, grinder, always fun and a giving soul."

"Keith Kimble: 'KK' has a brilliant future. A man of conviction. He relied on me to help him and I liked to do it. He will work a dozen Final Four's."

"Steve Gordon: My best pal in officiating and in life. We can talk and talk about our kids and our lives and then not talk for three months and then pick up right where we left off. One of the finest people I have ever met. Way underrated as an official. He was tremendous to work with. We have been there for each other through thick and thin. Just like best friends should be."

•••••

I had the good fortune to be a part of some of the great rebuilding jobs ever done in intercollegiate athletics. I was assistant AD at Northwestern during a 33 game football losing streak and was there for three great years when the rebuilding process started. That was fun. Doug Single was my boss and he taught me so much.

I was at Bucknell when we were able to get the football program back on track and win a championship that no one thought possible. When I went to Northern Iowa, the program was down in many areas. We (a great staff) and some of the best coaches ever got things fixed. I was able to hire Mark Farley as the Head Football Coach at UNI and together we took that program to the national championship game and he was named national coach of the year. I hired Bobbi Petersen and she took a volleyball program that was really good and made it — into a perennial national top 20 program. She was named national coach of the year. Chris Bucknam coached track for us, and he is the best coach I have ever seen at any level; he now is at Arkansas, what a great job he did and what a great friend he is. I hired Greg McDermott (Doug's dad) to coach UNI basketball. In our first game at the school together there were 228 people in the UNI-Dome to see us play. I know, I counted them. We were 6-25 the year before he came. In four years, we were in the NCAA tournament. And, we went three times in the next four years. He went on to Iowa State (I told him not to go!) and then to Creighton, and his son Doug became national player of the year. We turned the UNI basketball program over to the next coach, Ben Jacobsen (Jake), and the rest is history. Jake is one of the best coaches in the country and has kept up and built on the level of excellence.

Along with some other coaches I have had such as Jeff Bzdelik, Lynn Kachmarik, Pat Flannery, Sid Jamieson, the great Art Gulden, Rick Heller, Tom Gadd, Tonya Warren and John Bermel, I have been fortunate to be around some of the country's best. Thanks to all of you. And, for all the kids you have helped, thanks from them as well.

•••••

I have always thought that it is good to do things that are hard. Or at least to try them, learn, find out, experience them. I tell my speaking audiences all the time: Stretch yourself, do something out of your comfort range, something that is hard that you might not be sure you can do. My son (Nate) and I raced go-carts when we lived in Pennsylvania. I wanted us to have a shared passion, and had always enjoyed stock car racing, both on the dirt and NASCAR. So, we bought a cart and went racing.

We had no idea what we were doing, but after a lot of hard work and a couple of years of experience, we did pretty well. We won a bunch of races. When we moved to Iowa, my former brother-in-law, Denny Osborn and his son Brad sold us a late dirt model race car. We went off and raced that. We had some success, we learned, we worked and we fought with each other, but we had fun. The competition is stiff. Guys who we hung out around had been doing this for 20+ years. It was hard, but rewarding.

Then, my wife Jill came along and she wanted to race. So, we got her a car up and running. Then we decided we would try to race bigger, nationally, with the World of Outlaws Late Model Series. Man, those guys are good. It was hard. We would work all week, drive all night Thursday to wherever the races were for the weekend, race two or three nights and drive home and then go to work on Monday, then get the cars (two of them) ready to go again the next week. The workload was enormous, the costs significant.

We had a limited amount of success, but in the end we learned that the work is outrageous; the competition knows exactly what it is doing; you can buy speed and success, but only to a certain point; you need to be prepared beyond prepared so nothing minor beats you; and you better be ready to be tired out. It was hard, but I would do it again in a minute. Jill learned and grew as a driver and did some amazing things. She did some things no other woman has ever done in dirt race car. I am proud of her for that, and proud that I had a part in that growth and success. No one thought we could do it and we did. There is something about racing, refereeing, playing ball, being an administrator, at least for me, that are in my DNA. Keeping busy and working hard were bred into me at an early age. So, the fun of the chase outweighed the cost of work and play, both physically and financially.

•••••

Late in April of 2004, my son Nate and I had our race car all ready to go for the start of the season. We had done all the work, late at night, and other than getting the motor to run, we were ready to start the season two weeks later. It was a miracle. So, I worked all day at UNI, and quickly came home to help him with the last piece of the puzzle, getting the motor to run and checking all the fluids and everything that goes with it. I had our annual athletic banquet that night, so we had to hurry. Bad, bad idea.

We turned the motor over and it would not fire. This happens a lot after the motor has been refreshed. So, I did what you do in that case, took some racing fuel and poured it in the carburetor to get the motor to fire. First attempt, a little backfire, but it tried to start. On the second attempt, it backfired again, but I had the cup of gas I was holding too close and the backfire lit the gas, my hand and arm on fire. I dropped the gas and the fire went up my leg and pants. I knew immediately I was in trouble.

I ran outside, stopped, dropped, and rolled and put the fire out and then immediately went to the shower to wash off. The burns on my hand were not too bad, but my lower left leg was not good. I washed off, and Nate took me to Sartori hospital in Cedar Falls.

The staff there was great. I did not think the burns were bad, just get some dressing on them and I would be fine. Oh, no. Not so fast. I asked the intern what time I could get out because I had a banquet I had to attend. He told me, "You are not going to any banquet, we are getting the helicopter and you are being life-flighted to Iowa City." So, I knew this was bad. Five days in the hospital and a skin graft operation later, I was on my way home. I was very lucky. I had great doctors in Iowa City. I had burned myself very badly. It was embarrassing. What did I learn? Do not mess with things you do not know exactly how to do. Be careful with gas and fire. Listen to your friends who do know how to do such things. And, don't be in a hurry. I learned and am just fine now, but it was a scary (and very painful) couple of months. Stupid.

•••••

At Bucknell, I had to change football coaches. Bucknell had a history of having trouble winning football games. In fact, from 1963 to 1998 they had no winning seasons. It was awful. I knew it could be fixed with the right coach and I did everything in my power to find the right guy. I had a brainstorm.

Mike Ditka was unemployed. His brother, Ash, had played at Bucknell. Mike was from western Pennsylvania, and he knew about Bucknell because he had played at Bucknell while at Pittsburgh. I was going to call him and tell him I wanted to talk to him about the Bucknell head football job. I couldn't pay a huge salary, but he was a football coach; he would have a great time coaching at Bucknell; we had great kids, a wonderful place to live; he would bring notoriety and we could recruit great student-athletes and we would have fun doing it.

So, I called him. I pitched him on the job. We talked for half an hour. He said, "Give me 48 hours and I will call you back." I waited. And, he called. And, he said he appreciated my thinking of him, but he just couldn't do it right now, at this place in his life. I tried. I tried to recruit the great Mike Ditka to coach the Bison. I ended up hiring Tom Gadd, who turned us into a winner. I am not sure anyone else could have done it. Tom was the best. But, having Iron Mike would have been a blast.

●●●●●

One year during football season at Bucknell, we played at our rival, Lehigh. We had a good team, and we had a chance to beat Lehigh, which did not happen often. It just so happened that we had some really good I-AA players, two of whom later played in the NFL. Those type of extremely bright and talented kids were hard to get at Bucknell.

Long story short, we were behind by 5 points, and were driving for the go ahead score, late in the game. Fourth down and three at the Lehigh 20 yard line. Timeout. I was standing on the sideline in hopes of being there to support the team and coach if we happened to win, or lose. I will never forget what took place. I had hired a very bright and cerebral coach, and good guy, Lou Maranzana. The kids loved Lou and he did a good job for us at Bucknell. We also had a very good wide receiver, Lester Erb, from Milton, PA, just across the river from Bucknell (who would later coach college football at several stops, including the University of Iowa). As the brain trust pondered just the right play, Lester was fidgeting, waiting, standing behind the coaches. I could tell he really wanted to give his input. He finally could not stand it any longer.

He stuck his head in the huddle and said, "Coach, we have an All-American running back (Brian Hennessey) and we have an All-American left tackle (Jay Butler) who is going to play in the ____damn NFL, pitch the ball to Hennessey and have him run behind Butler and we will make the _____ing first down and then we will win the game." A pretty bold statement, I thought. And, that is what they decided to do. And, we made the first down. And, we drove for a touchdown to win the game. And, beat the dreaded Lehigh Engineers. Good call, Lester. That is leadership.

• • • • •

2008 was Jim "Boomer" Bain's last year as Missouri Conference Men's Basketball Supervisor of Officials. I was fortunate enough to work the regular season conference championship game for Boomer that year, Illinois State at Creighton. It was Boomer's last game as a supervisor. We worked a terrific game. It was a great finish for him. He was so proud of us. The three officials and Boomer stood together in that locker room in Omaha and hugged and cried. "I am so proud that you guys were here to work this game. You were just awesome. You let this old guy go out on the highest note ever. Thank you." Those were Boomer's words. I have never been more proud. We carried the mail for Boomer.

• • • • •

I would be totally remiss if I did not mention the person and coach who had a huge influence in my life, Coach Virgil Goodrich. Virg was my neighbor as I grew up on the farm in Klemme, Iowa. He came back to Klemme to teach and coach after college. He was my football coach, and taught me that I could dream bigger, accomplish more than I thought, coming out of a tiny farm town in north central Iowa. My dad was sick. Virg was my second dad. Thank you, coach, for giving me the inspiration and confidence to try and make something of myself. I would never have tried without you making me believe I could do it.

• • • • •

Why do people go into athletics as a career? Why in the world do they officiate games? I think the answers are because those gyms and those fields are where they are most comfortable in life. I know with me that's the case. That is where you belong. That is where you have learned life's best lessons and where you have enjoyed some of life's greatest moments. So, when you cannot play anymore, or when you have had enough of coaching, then administration or officiating are the ways you can stay in the arena, stay involved, give back, be comfortable, and still be a part of what is deeply embedded in your soul — the need to compete and chase the dream of doing better, giving your best and working so hard and then collapsing at the end of the day knowing that you gave your all in an area that you love and that after you rest a little you will ready to do it again tomorrow. The competition drives us all who are involved in athletics. Not just the competition to win or to prove you are the best, but the competition that allows you to be the best you can possibly become and then see how that stacks up against all the others. It's the people and the journey, not the winning that keeps us working in the athletics arena.

●●●●●

I grew up on 240 mediocre acres in a quintessential Iowa farm community. My dad and mom pounded out a living on that ground by raising corn and beans, oats and hay. We raised cattle, pigs and chickens, and occasionally a few sheep. We also milked about 20 head of dairy cattle. It was a hard life, but we did not know how hard. We were poor, but we had food on the table and love in our hearts for our little family, my mom (Neva) and dad (Bob) and my sister (Jody). It was a great way to grow up. I would not trade it for anything. It was innocent and far from the big cities and bright lights, but it had an innocence and "our own little world" sort of feel.

I can never forget baling hay in the heat of the summer or milking those cows on a frigid winter day, watching baby pigs born or your family dog die in front of you. Or watching my dad stand at the kitchen counter and cry when it hailed and ruined all of our crops. It was a life that shaped me, taught me that the only way to succeed is through hard, hard work and to have a passion in your gut that will not let you fail.

The greatest basketball court of all time was on that farm. My dad put up a backboard and hoop in our barn. When we baled hay and put it in the barn, he would let me place the bales in a manner that kept the court available, even though it was small, so I could practice my shooting year round. As we used the hay to feed the cattle and cows, my court grew. By late winter there would be a full indoor half court, which was kept warm by the hay surrounding it and the heat from the cows just below my upstairs court. It does not get any better than that. My mom often told me that all the way through high school she never worried about where I was because she could hear the bounce of the ball in the barn and knew I was safe and sound and where she could find me.

Our town was tiny, 600 residents. Our farm was two miles west of Klemme, Iowa. The Shamrocks were our mascot, even though I do not know of one Irish person who lived there. The school was the centerpiece of the town, and our sports teams, band and choir, plays and other school activities, along with two strong churches, kept the town alive.

Thirty-six kids were in our graduating class, the biggest class ever out of old KHS. I got a great education there. The teachers and administrators and coaches cared about all the students. We had good, not great, athletic success. But that town and that school prepared me well to go out into the world, and for that I am thankful.

Like so many Midwest towns whose population decreases, the school in my home town is gone now — consolidated with the dreaded town of Belmond. Belmond-Klemme, they call it. The Broncos are the mascot. Not me. It is Klemme for me and always will be. That is my hometown, and I am proud to say I was raised there and so are a number of people like me who went through places like that and know that the way of life we grew up with was innocent, yet special — not to be duplicated in the current day and age, no matter how hard we try.

•••••

Just as my friend Dave Simon and I were putting this book to bed and getting ready to send it to the editor for the final review, I got a chance to go back and visit my old hometown, with my dear friend, Jim 'Speedy' Thomas and his wife Teri. Speedy and I were football playing teammates at UNI, then we coached together at Coe College. I was there when Teri and Speedy met, got married, and had their first child. Speedy's grandpa, Jim, was my barber when I was growing up and he spent a lot of time in the tiny town of Klemme, staying with his grandpa and grandma. So, we took a road trip on the occasion of the reunion of the 1975 UNI Football team. We had talked about this many times, so doing it together to have a chance to relive all the old memories was fun.

We talked and laughed on the hour-and-a-half trip home. It was a great time. We went by the old farmhouse where I was raised. There was a "For Sale" sign on the house and no one around, so we pulled in the driveway and looked around. I am dealing with so many emotions now after having gone back to see my old place. Of course, I had driven past it many times over the years.

My mom and sister moved out of the farm after my dad died, so it has been a long time since we lived there. But, it was in such bad shape. The barn where I played and worked had fallen down. Oh, the memories I have of that barn, for so many reasons. Hard, hard work. Stacking the hay; milking the cows; cleaning up the manure and all that goes with livestock. And, the great basketball court, which I have described elsewhere in this book. The corn crib had fallen down, as had the hog barn. Our machine shed was still there, albeit in bad shape. I went around the house and looked in all the windows at the rooms where I grew up; where I ate and slept and played.

My knees buckled when Speedy asked me where we put our Christmas tree. I remember the Christmas time there so vividly. Long story made short, I lived a beautiful childhood. What a fantastic place to live and grow up. And nearly every single memory of that farm is good for me. But the lawn where I played football was now way too small and covered with weeds; the barn where I played and where I pitched baseball against the cement had gone away. The acreage was overgrown and unkempt and it made me sad. It was "my place" and now it was so much different. I guess it is a rite of passage for each of us to have to relive those memories and great times; and, I will get over it, but what a great life that was. Innocent. The world was so small and harmless. We were poor but we had it made. And, I miss those days so terribly.

•••••

Just as this book was going to our final editor, a small tragedy occurred. I had the cover picture for the book shot at my neighbor's horse barn, which is just down the gravel road from my house. In fact, I bought my house from Trudy and her husband Dennis, when I came back to Cedar Falls in 2000. Trudy and Dennis had built a new and fabulous horse facility and house, so they sold me their old one. Dennis passed away last year and Trudy has been running her barn and raising and training her horses by herself. Trudy is a fabulous person, salt of the earth, a tough and strong and resilient woman. She has become a great friend to my family and to me and we all love her. Trudy was moving some things in the upper level of her barn the other night and somehow fell from the upper level to the concrete floor below. As I write, she is at the University of Iowa Hospital being treated for her injuries, which are significant. She has gone through one surgery and even though the reports are encouraging, we do not know how she will come through this incident. But, I am betting on Trudy on this one. She is tough and strong and resilient and we have seen that over and over in her life. I know this: we all will do everything we can to help her while she recovers. You get better my friend! Get back on that horse again. We all are rooting for you and for a full recovery.

•••••

Dave Simon, who did such great work helping me get this book going and ultimately done, found a tremendous editor who has made the final product of this book possible and has been so wonderful in the process. Dave found Janet Long, of Richardson, Texas, to do the editing and layout. I cannot tell you how great she has been to work with and how understanding and flexible she has been as we have tried to bring this book to a close. Thank you, Janet. You are the best!

•••••

When my wife Kathy and I were first married, in 1977, we both knew we wanted to have children. I had been raised by great parents, and so had Kathy, and we wanted to share our love with our own kids in the same way we were taught and raised. After a couple of years we decided to give it a try. We found out that we had a problem and probably could not have kids of our own. That was tough to learn, but we decided immediately to see if we could adopt a child and to build our family that way. I spent every day for nearly two years working on this adoption process. We investigated every option, and finally ended up working with a group called Concern For Children, out of Ohio. The people there were great to work with, very helpful. We went through the entire process necessary to adopt, and it is an extensive and exhausting process.

I was in touch with our state representatives and congressmen, trying to move the never-ending process along. We were told we were 20th in line for a Central American adoption, and that we should expect to wait several years for the process to be complete. So, we were patient. Then, all of a sudden, and without warning, in December of 1980, we got a call from the agency which was helping, and said they had found a little boy for us, about eight months old, in El Salvador. They would send a picture and details.

When we got the picture, it was a Polaroid taken from about six inches away, and all we could see was half of the face of the little boy who was to be ours. But, there was no idea when we could get him. So, we waited some more. Then on December 19, 1980, the call came that we needed to be in San Salvador (capital of country of El Salvador) on January 3, 1981, some two weeks later. We were school teachers and we did not have the money necessary to pay the agency, get all the documents necessary and travel to San Salvador. So, on December 31 we jumped in our car and drove from Iowa to New Orleans. From there we were to fly to San Salvador, to pick up our boy.

We were only told a few things. We would be there three days. It was a dangerous time in El Salvador, they were in the midst of a civil war. We were given a hotel to report to and the name of the social worker in San Salvador, whom we were to contact when we got there. And, we were told to go immediately to the United States Embassy in San Salvador when we arrived, so they knew we were there. (And, I assume, that if we went missing, they would know that too). And, we were told to book the first flight of the day out of New Orleans so we would land in San Salvador in the daylight. No problem, we could do all these things.

So, the adventure began. Everything was going along smoothly until our original plane was cancelled on Taca Airlines and we got on the next available plane; we landed at the San Salvador airport at midnight. Oh-oh. No one spoke English. There were soldiers with guns all over the place. We had no idea what to do. How do we get to the hotel? Can we get through Customs somehow? I saw some flight attendants whom I thought might speak English so Kathy and I went to them to ask for advice.

What happened was crazy; they told us they were going to another hotel in San Salvador, that we should not be traveling alone and to get into their van with them. We skipped Customs, and went with them. We drove out of the airport, which is in the middle of the country and up a two lane, blacktop road. You could hear gun battles taking place. We stopped twice on our way to the hotel to allow activity to take place on the road, then we drove into the city. We were dropped off at our hotel.

The next morning we called the U.S. Embassy and our social worker. We were told where to meet him, at a place called Pete's Donuts (I swear you could not make this up!) and we met him there. He took us to a church where there must have been 400 kids running all over the church and its property. These kids were from two months to 18 years old, all awaiting adoption or placement. We walked down the aisle of the church to go to the Director's office. There were dozens of small children in cribs. As we turned the corner to head to the office, I stopped and rubbed the head of a little boy who was crawling in his crib. I just couldn't help myself.

We met the Director, did all the paperwork we had to do and then were told we could go meet our son. We walked out of the office and went directly to the crib of the little boy whose head I had rubbed on the way to the office. That was our little boy, whom we named Nathaniel Robert (Nate) Hartzell. I fell to my knees. Kathy was emotional as well. This was a full-fledged miracle. Nate had been born in a jungle and brought to the church by someone in his small town; they literally saved his life and gave us a chance to come and get him and bring him to the United States with us.

In order to get Nate out of the country, we had to go to the U.S. Embassy and sign some papers and then we had to see a lawyer from the El Salvador government. The paperwork at the Embassy was not an issue. But, when we saw the lawyer, she told us that she would not release Nate to us, because they were certain that he had some serious health problems. He only weighed 12 pounds at nine months old, and they thought he had tuberculosis. Fortunately, the lawyer spoke excellent English. I explained to her that we lived two hours from the best hospital in the world, the Mayo Clinic, and that we would get Nate to that hospital the day we got home. Please, let him come home with us, it is his only chance. I pleaded and begged. And, she said yes, and signed the release papers.

We then went to see a doctor who quickly examined Nate, gave us some medicine to give him when we got to the airport, and signed the release papers. We were good to take Nate home and we started that journey home the next day, with our precious bundle of joy in tow. As instructed, when we got to the airport, we gave Nate the medicine. He immediately started going to the bathroom at a record setting rate. We made it on the plane and the bathroom problem continued. I was in the bathroom of the plane changing his diaper as the plane proceeded down the runway. I made it to my seat, as we took off. We made it to Guatemala to stay overnight, then to New Orleans, then the drive home.

What an incredible adventure. We got Nate home, took him to our family doctor immediately and it was determined that he had a milk allergy. And, since all they had fed him in El Salvador was milk and jello, it was no wonder he was such a little bit of thing when we got him. We got him off milk, put him on a milk substitute and he took off. I don't think he has been sick a day in his life since then.

What did we learn from this adventure and ordeal?

1) That miracles do happen, and there is no doubt about that.
2) That we did something great to help a beautiful young boy have an opportunity to have a wonderful life (and he has done just that).
3) That if you are resilient and tough and you don't give up, you can do something that no one thought possible, and get through all the red tape to help another person.
(4) That my faith in God would never waiver after the little boy's head who I rubbed on the way by his crib became my son and my life-long friend.
5) And, that while sometimes scared, apprehensive, and un-

sure of what would happen next and how we would get this done, we had faith that a higher power "had our back."

I am so proud that Kathy and I did this. I am proud that we didn't quit on the process and that we hung in there and brought home a little boy who has grown into a wonderful young man.

•••••

This book has covered a lot of ground. One of the things I did not do a chapter on was faith. I know that is uncomfortable ground for some people and some authors. It is not uncomfortable for me; I have great faith in a higher power, one much greater than me. I hope that everyone has faith like that, but I am not preaching here nor telling anyone how they should live. I believe in God and I believe that Jesus Christ died for our sins. I have always had good faith, and was raised in a Christian home where you believed, went to church every Sunday (even if the Chicago Bears kickoff was imminent) and acted in a way that represented that faith.

Some of that faith slipped over the years. But there is good news! I found Prairie Lakes Church in Cedar Falls, and Pastor John Fuller and Gabe Berger. They are wonderful men, and the church welcomes anyone, regardless of where you have been and what you have done. The church has changed my life by bringing me peace and comfort. I have crossed the "faith line" as we say at Prairie Lake, and it has made such a significant difference that I felt compelled to write these words. In my opinion, until you have heard Pastor John at his finest, you have not lived. That faith and belief system is a part of me now, and proud to be able to write it down. Thank you for indulging me on this matter.

FAVORITE QUOTES, SAYINGS AND INSPIRATIONAL THOUGHTS

- Never be afraid to try something new. Remember, amateurs built the arc. Professionals built the Titanic.

- There is no elevator to success. You have to take the stairs.

- It is not who you are that keeps you back, it is who you think you are not. So, start believing in yourself.

- Though no one can go back and make a brand new start, anyone can start from now and make a brand new ending.

- I have learned that the easiest way for me to grow as a person is to make sure that I surround myself with people who are smarter than I am.

- I have learned that when you are in love, it shows. So, start loving life, your job, your family and all those around you — it makes a huge difference!

- The greatest pleasure in life is doing what other people say you cannot do.

- There is no telling how many miles you will have to run while chasing a dream.

- The mark of a successful man is one who has spent an entire day on the bank of a river and does not feel guilty about it.

- There is a difference between interest and commitment. When you are interested in doing something, you do it only when circumstances permit. When you are committed to something you do not accept excuses, only results.

- Ever had a ham and cheese omelet? The chicken was interested. The pig was committed.

- To reach a great height, a person needs to have great depth.

- Forgiveness is all about me giving up my right to hurt you for hurting me.

- A successful person is one who can lay a solid foundation with the bricks others have thrown at him.

- If you face severe hardships in life and you do not surrender, that shows strength.

- Always be above the fray. Take the high road at all times.

- It is nice to be important. It is more important to be nice.

- Great minds discuss ideas, average minds discuss events, small minds discuss people.

- If there is anything that we wish to change in a child, we should first examine it and see if it is something we could better change in ourselves.

- Live each day as you would want to live the last day of your life.

- Bad habits are evil inclinations acquired through repeated bad acts. Unless we overcome these habits they will become our master.

- Great people are just ordinary people with an extraordinary amount of determination.

- What I am is God's gift to me; what I make of myself is my gift to Him.

- Get rid of the people in your life who tell you what you cannot do.

- Life's currency is the friends we make.

- Approach every day at work like it is your first day and every day with your family like it is your last.

- Never stop trying to see what else in life you are good at doing.

- Things turn out best for people who make the best out of the way things turn out.

- People don't care about how much you know until they know about how much you care.

- If you do not have goals, or energy or passion or an interest in doing more or doing better then this life and this world is just a "waiting room" for you.

- "You are the only one who will really know whether you made the effort to do the best of what you are capable." ~ John Wooden

- The greatest of successes you will ever attain are still waiting for you on the road ahead.

- Every person has within themselves an inexhaustible reserve of potential they have never even come close to realizing.

- "Nothing will test your faith like a long sermon on a pretty Sunday." ~ Brad Paisley

- "Life is not tried; it is merely survived if you are standing outside the fire." ~ Garth Brooks

- "Great" is made by standing on the back of "good."

- The measure of success is not whether you have a tough problem to deal with but rather whether it is the same problem you had last year.

- "Your success is not determined by your talent or skill, but by your will." ~ Vince Lombardi

- Listening is the act of generously making space for what someone else has to say and doing it without resistance.

- If you can hold your head up with a smile on your face, you are truly blessed because most people can do that but choose not to.

- A home without a child is like a wound without salt.

- Successful people always make logical and informed decisions.

- Failure is a bruise, not a tattoo.

- Work like you don't need the money. Love like you have never been hurt. Dance like nobody is watching.

- "Success is the peace of mind which is direct result of self-satisfaction in knowing you did your best to become the best that you are capable of becoming." ~ John Wooden

- Somehow along the course of life you learn about yourself and realize there should never be regrets, only a lifelong appreciation of the choices you have made.

- There comes a time when we have to stop loving someone not because that person has stopped loving us but because we have found out that they would be happier if we let go.

- There is nothing better than riding in the bed of a pickup on a warm Iowa night.

- I believe that you can keep going long after you think you can't.

- I believe that money is a lousy way of keeping score.

- I believe that it is taking me a long time to become the person I want to be.

- You should never waste an opportunity to tell someone you love them.

- You should never expect life to be fair.

- Live your life as an exclamation not as an explanation.

- "Art and science have their meeting point in method." ~ Edward G. Bullwer-Lytton

- Stop telling God how big your storm is. Instead, tell your storm how big your God is.

- Expect to be exceptional.

- Mediocrity is excellence to the mediocre.

- You know you are from Iowa if you know the answer to the question, "is this heaven?"

- "Mankind has never advanced a centimeter by hating or showing prejudice. We only make advancements when we have been brothers and sisters at labor toward a common goal." ~ Dale Brown

- "The best potential of me, is we." ~ Dale Brown

- "A person gets his or her identity in life based on how the most important person in his life sees him." ~ Richard Simmons III

- I have learned that everyone wants to live on top of the mountain but all the happiness and growth occurs while you are climbing it.

- The people who are hardest to love...need your love the most.

- Our background and circumstances influence who we are, but we are responsible for who we become.

- Just because someone does not love you the way you want them to does not mean they don't love you with all they have.

- Measure twice, cut once.

- You didn't come this far to only come this far.

- I can do all things through Christ, who strengthens me. ~ *Philippians 4:13*

I have used the following story many times in my motivational speaking engagements and people seem to really like it, so I am reproducing it here.

THE CARPENTER

An elderly carpenter was ready to retire. He told his employer, a contractor, of his plans to leave the house building business to live a more leisurely life with his wife and extended family. He would miss the paycheck, but he needed to retire. They could get by.

The contractor was sorry to see his good worker go and asked if he could build just one more house as a personal favor. The carpenter said "Yes," but in time it was easy to see that his heart just was not in his work. He resorted to shoddy workmanship and used inferior materials. It was an unfortunate way to end a dedicated career.

When the carpenter finished his work and the house was done, the employer came by to inspect the house. He then handed the front door key to the carpenter. "This is your house," he said, "my gift to you."

The carpenter was shocked. What a shame! If he had only known he was building his own house he would have done it so much differently.

And, so it is with us. We build our lives, one day at a time, often putting less than our best effort into the building. Then with shock we realize we have to live in the house we have built. Then we realize that if we could go back and do it all over again we would do it much differently. But, we cannot go back.

You are the carpenter. Each day you hammer a nail, place a board or erect a wall. "Life is a do-it-yourself project," someone once said. Your attitudes and the choices you make today will build the house you will live in tomorrow. Build wisely!

Remember..."Work like you don't need the money. Dance like no one is watching. Love like you have never been hurt."

Author Unknown

THANK YOU

I would like to offer a special "thank you" to Mike Krzyzewski for writing the foreword to this book. It was scary thinking of who might be the best to do the foreword. Obviously, Coach K was a no-brainer, but I was not sure he would have the time, or the interest to do it. I was amazed, frankly, when he answered back and told me he would be honored and privileged to write the foreword to endorse this book. I have always held Coach K in the highest regard. He has brought so many positive qualities to college basketball that they are too many to list. His teams play extremely hard, they compete every night, they play with class and respect. Those qualities reflect their coach.

I will never forget, I was at Duke one night and called a foul on a young, first-year player. He said to me, "Mr. Hartzell, can you explain to me what I did for you to call that foul?" I explained what I saw, and he replied with a "thank you." It's very unusual for a player to know an official's name. That player was Carlos Boozer. A few years later, Shane Battier did the very same thing. I think that tells you what the Duke basketball program, and Mike Krzyzewski, are all about. I am honored and privileged to have Coach K do the foreword for this book. I am forever indebted. Thank you to the best coach that college and Olympic basketball have ever seen.

I would also like to thank the outstanding basketball people and coaches who endorsed this book for me by putting their quotes of support on the back cover. They are:

- Dick Vitale, the long-time ESPN announcer who, in the opinion of many, has done more to promote college basketball than anyone else. Dick has always been gracious and supportive and he lent his endorsement without question.

- Fran Fraschilla, another ESPN announcer and former coach whose games I worked at St. John's and New Mexico. By the way, Fran is easier to get along with now than he was when he coached! He is a friend and a huge supporter of my officiating brethren.

- Bill Self, the outstanding Kansas coach. He has won national championships and league titles too numerous to mention and we have had our moments of conflict, but he is a pro, a champion, and a really, really good man.

- Steve Gordon, an excellent referee and friend, and my "best man." Steve is the best person ever and his endorsement of this book means the world to me.

- Greg McDermott, current head coach at Creighton University. I hired Mac at UNI and he took the job when no one thought it was any good nor could it be. Six years and 3 NCAA tournaments later, everyone knew it was a good job.

- Ben Jacobson, the current head coach at Northern Iowa. I hired him to follow Mac and while I knew he would be good, I never knew he would be this good. Widely considered one of the top 20 coaches in the country, his endorsement carries great meaning to me personally.

- I would like to offer a special "thank you" to Janet Long, of Richardson, Texas, who did a simply outstanding job in the editing of this book. She put up with several changes, and revisions, and changes in direction and was as professional as anyone could ever be in her work. We could not have done this without you.

RICK HARTZELL
MAJOR LIFE ACCOMPLISHMENTS

- Graduate of Klemme, Iowa, High School. 36 kids in graduating class.

- 5 sport and 18 varsity letter winner; All-state in football, basketball and baseball

- Played football and baseball at UNI

- Graduate of UNI with two degrees, B.A. (English and PE), M.A. (Educational Administration)

- Two years of high school teaching at Fredericksburg, Iowa, and Tri-County High School

- Graduate Assistant Football Coach at UNI, 1977-78

- Teacher and Coach at Coe College, Cedar Rapids, IA, 1977-80. Assistant football coach and head baseball coach. National baseball coach of the year, Division III, 1978

- Doctoral student and assistant baseball coach, University of Iowa, 1980-82. Doctoral work in Higher Education Administration, comprehensive exam complete, (ABD)

- Assistant Athletic Director, Northwestern University, 1982-85

- Director of Athletics, University of Maryland at Baltimore, 1985-88

- Director of Athletics, Bucknell University, Lewisburg, PA, 1988-99

- Director of Athletics, University of Northern Iowa, Cedar Falls, IA, 1999-2008

- ACC Basketball Commissioner's Award, 1995

- National AD of the Year while at UNI, 2008
- Elected to the Iowa Fastpitch Softball Hall of Fame, 2005
- Elected to the UNI School of HPERD Hall of Achievement, 2004
- CEO at Three Wide Media, 2008-present
- Owner of RickHartzell.com, Motivational Speaking Business, 2008-present
- President, Missouri Valley Director's of Athletics, 2004
- Member, NCAA Basketball Rules Committee, 2008
- Dad to Nate, Amanda, Jackson and Jace
- Officiated major college basketball since 1982 in the following NCAA Division I leagues: Mid-American, Big Ten, ACC, Big East, SEC, Pac 12, Mountain West, WAC, West Coast, Horizon League, Colonial, East Coast Athletic Conference, Southern, Sun Belt, Missouri Valley. Highlights include 21 NCAA tournaments, 25 conference championship games, NIT Championship Game. Officiated over 3,500 games at the Division I level, more than 4,300 games total.

Dave Simon officiated basketball for 18 years, 12 at the small college level. He started in the Washington, D.C. metro area, and after 13 years, he took a job in Nebraska, and continued blowing the whistle for five more years before the demands of his full-time job made it impossible to continue.

Dave began his writing career as a reporter in Washington, D.C., covering environmental issues before the U.S. Congress and Environmental Protection Agency. He began writing for *Referee Magazine* over 25 years ago, and writes several stories for the publication every year, often focusing on basketball.

He writes a weekly social commentary column that has run in newspapers in Nebraska, Illinois, Pennsylvania and Texas. Dave also wrote *Bad Golf* available electronically through Barnes and Noble and Amazon. It is a humorous take about life on the links. He writes a cooking blog, a writing tips blog and a *Bad Golf* blog, all available on his Web site, www.justwrite15.com.

Rick Hartzell grew up in rural Iowa, on a farm, where he was taught that the only way to survive was through hard work. He learned the value of family, solid values and faith. A gym rat at heart, Hartzell has been around athletics in one form or another all of his life.

He played football, basketball, baseball and softball, earning accolades and honors in each. He began his athletic administration career at Northwestern University and that work took him to the University of Maryland-Baltimore, Bucknell University and the University of Northern Iowa. He helped build championship programs at each stop. In addition, he has refereed Division I men's basketball games since 1982 in all of the major conferences, including over 20 years in the ACC, Big 10, and Big 12. He has worked over 3,500 games, 23 NCAA tournaments, 25 NIT tournaments and numerous conference championship games.

Hartzell currently is CEO of Three Wide Media and runs a successful public speaking and motivational speaking business, www.RickHartzell.com.

Some words from Rick: It is really hard to believe (the born and raised and darn proud of it Iowa farm boy) that I have attempted to write a book. People from where I come from do not write books. By my own personal research, I am the first to do so other than the annual Methodist Women's Cookbook, which is produced annually by some of the greatest cooks the world has ever seen. So, as far as I know, this is the first attempt at a real book by someone who grew up in my hometown of Klemme, Iowa. I am writing this book for several key reasons:

- I want to leave something for my four wonderful children to remember me by. Nate, Amanda, Jackson and Jace, this effort, more than anything else, is for you. I love you. Family and eternity are all that really matter to me, and maybe someday you can sit down and read a part of this book to your kids or your grandkids or someone you love, and smile when you are doing it, knowing that it came from your dad.

- I thank the Lord for giving me enough talent to write the words in this book. So many people have encouraged me to try and do this over the years, and even though I am not so sure that they thought I could do it, here is my effort to show them.

- I have always thought that people who write books must be really smart, but I found out while writing this book that persistence may well be the more important quality. Obviously, this book-writing effort will prove that hypothesis wrong. Persistent maybe, but not very smart.

- Even though I was raised where I was raised, and have gone through my share of life's hard lessons, I have learned a great deal in this life well-lived and I want to be able to share it in my particular style.

- Hopefully this book helps the reader live a better life — a very simple goal. If I accomplish that goal, then this work has been worth every hour and sleepless night.